Papa is the sky
Mama is the air
Elaina is the clouds
Zoya is the moon
And Polly is the sun

– Zoya, age 5

D1502636

SUN SHINE DOWN

a memoir

gillian marchenko

ts T. S. Poetry Press • New York

T. S. Poetry Press
Ossining, New York
Tspoetry.com

This memoir includes various references from or to the following brands & sources: Disney brand, The Walt Disney Company; Styrofoam brand, The Dow Chemical Company; *E.T.*, Directed by Steven Speilberg, 1982; *Myths and Truths about Down syndrome*, The National Down Syndrome Society; Pepto-Bismol brand, Proctor and Gamble Manufacturing Company; *Jewel*, by Bret Lott, Washington Square Press, 1999; *Mork and Mindy*, Created by Gary Marshall, 1978 to 1982; Elmer's Glue brand, Elmer's Products, Inc.; Polly Pocket brand, Mattel; Strawberry Shortcake brand, American Greetings; Crayola brand, Crayola LLC; Google Inc.; www.downsyn.com, by Thomas and Michel Paul, 1997 to 2008; Canada Dry brand, Dr Pepper Snapple Group; Target Inc.; *Law and Order: Special Victims Unit*, Created by Dick Wolf, 1999; Wal-Mart Inc.; *Babies with Down Syndrome: A New Parent's Guide*, edited by Karen Stray-Gundersen, Woodbine House, second edition, 1995; NBC commercials, NBC: General Electric; *Cheaper By The Dozen*, Directed by Shawn Levy, 2003; *Chitty Chitty Bang Bang*, Directed by Ken Hughes, 1968; *Stuart Little*, Directed by Rob Minkoff, 1999; The "Electric Slide", by Rick Silver, 1976; *We'll Paint the Octopus Red*, by Stephanie Stuve-Bodeen (Author), Pam Devito (Illustrator), Woodbine House, 1998; Princess Leia brand, The Walt Disney Company.

Some names and contexts have been changed to protect the privacy of individuals.

Cover image by Kelly Sauer. kellysauer.com

ISBN 978-0-9898542-0-7

Library of Congress Cataloging-in-Publication Data:
Marchenko, Gillian
       [Memoir.]
       Sun Shine Down/Gillian Marchenko
       ISBN 978-0-9898542-0-7
       Library of Congress Control Number: 2013947901

for Polly

Prologue

The summer before second grade I thought God ripped my arm off to teach me a lesson.

It happened on the playground at Cardinal Field—the social hub of Dryden, the small town in the thumb of Michigan where I grew up with my cousins. We were trying to make a fort out of two tractor tires near the swing set. I was the oldest at seven. Gary was six, Jason was five, and little Mandy could not have been more than three. Jason and I shared a birthday, March 2, which in our minds made us smarter than the others. How clever of us to be born the same day.

Working together, we lifted one tractor tire and started to roll it to the other tire. "Hold it this way, Jason," I admonished my tow-headed cousin. "Mandy, stay back!" Gary told his sister. It was all very serious. We had a job to do. I held the tire from the left side and Gary and Jason stood on the right. After moving a foot or so, the tall tire came crashing down on me. I lay there, my body flung out, my left arm pinned. I tried to wiggle my fingers, but I couldn't feel anything.

"Mandy, go tell my mom I ripped my arm off!"
My cousin's eyes looked like two empty white cups. She started to cry and took off into the fields, as her brothers bent down to lift the tire. "Leave it," I said. "My mom will be here in a minute." A sharp pain pulsed through my shoulder. The ground seemed to freeze like a Minnesota lake in the dead of winter.

I waited for help and thought about Daniel, a boy who wore a prosthetic. Daniel's leg wasn't like the rest of ours. He'd clank and clatter when he'd play tag, walking as fast as he could, trying to pass it off as a run. A thick leather strap looped down his leg and under his shoe.

One day at school I came out of the girls' bathroom and stopped to get a drink from the water fountain. I noticed Daniel on the ground, wedged between the large, steel boys' bathroom door and its frame, naked except for his white underwear.

When I saw him, I looked away—because of his underwear and because a knobbed leg stuck out, the other full leg tucked behind him out of sight.

"Help me," Daniel pleaded. Crying, he fixed his eyes on me. My mother had taught me not to stare, but his lack of a leg fascinated me. It stopped where a knee should be, rounded, smooth. I knew something was different about Daniel's leg; all the kids in our class did. But I didn't realize it was gone. A mixture of nausea and fear washed over me, and I turned and started back towards class. "Please, help me! Please!"

I slipped into the classroom. Kids worked on math problems at their desks. I sidled up to the teacher's desk, returned the hall pass, and made my way to my seat. No one knew Daniel was wedged between the wall and the large steel bathroom door. What did I just see? How did he get stuck? I tried to wipe Daniel out of my mind. But every time I closed my eyes I saw him. I was afraid to tell my teacher he was naked and stuck, half way out of the bathroom. I was afraid to tell anyone he didn't have the bottom part of his leg.

A few minutes later a student from another class poked her head into the room and told the teacher about Daniel. "Class, keep working!" She rushed out. Kids started talking and laughing and acting up. I stared down at my wide-ruled paper and gripped my pencil.

The morning the tire tractor pinned me to the ground, my older brother came through the field, pulled the tire off and carried me home. Pain ripped through my arm. *God was punishing me for not helping Daniel.*

My mom inspected my swollen shoulder—its piece of bone sticking out—then rushed me to the hospital. My left arm was broken. The doctor had kind eyes and huge, soft hands. He explained my operation; I would take medicine that would help me sleep, and he would fix my arm and then wake me back up. One of his large hands rested near me while he talked— his fingernail beds perfect half-moons.

Two hours later, I woke up in a room with Disney characters painted on the walls in red, blue, green and yellow. I noticed my arm was casted from shoulder to wrist. Somewhere, I have a black and white picture of me in the room. I look small and sullen, drinking ginger ale out of a tall Styrofoam® cup with a straw. I remember being surprised I still had two arms.

Before seeing Daniel, I did not know there were people in the world without things like legs. Broken people existed. What a frightening discovery.

I woke up just before seven the morning of April 5, 2006, in a surgical recovery room in a hospital in Kiev, Ukraine. Sluggish, I scanned the room, unable to take in my surroundings. A thin white sheet covered my body. I shivered. A metal table housed a tiny television in the corner of the room. The bare walls were a pale shade of blue gray.

Did Sergei leave? Lifting my hand, I placed it on my breast-bone and slid it towards my navel. My mid-section felt numb. Pushing down, it was as if I tapped another person's toneless stomach. White gauze held my empty abdomen tight. I had been eight months pregnant.

Five hours earlier, I stood naked in a warm shower, my blond hair tucked into a flimsy paper cap. A delivery nurse crouched in front of my middle. "Krasata," she hummed in Russian, smiling, telling me I was beautiful, while methodically shaving me.

I couldn't see the nurse's face over the bulge of my stomach. Her brown hair bobbed in and out of sight as she talked. I imagined her gold tooth sparkling as her mouth moved. In Russian, *krasata* means *beautiful* as in, *you are a beauty*. My skin was now translucent, stretched to its limit. I looked like ET's pregnant cousin, wide-eyed from fear, hair thinned.

"Tebye nada peesat?" the nurse asked as she cleaned off the razor. I nodded — *yes, I have to pee,* and then I squatted, awkward, as my bladder emptied. I hadn't peed in front of someone since kindergarten, when I used to make my best friend, Carol Peruski, go to the bathroom with me. The yellow stream swirled around and around the shower floor before sliding down the drain. I wanted to be back home in Michigan, tucked away in an American hospital. I wanted to understand everything being said to me.

I had hugged my daughters goodbye that morning, expecting to return in a few hours. Elaina, five and a half years old, had a habit of patting my tummy hello and goodbye. Zoya, eighteen months younger, stood on her tiptoes and aligned her lips with my belly button for a kiss. They hurried our departure. They had big plans to make a fort underneath the dining room table with their beloved Ukrainian nanny, Lena.

Our *stalinka*—the historical apartment in Kiev where we'd been living for the last three years, since we'd moved from Chicago to Sergei's native Ukraine to help start and grow churches—showed few signs of a baby coming. A pack of diapers and some second-hand clothes were piled in the corner. A stroller stood in the hallway by the front door next to a line of shoes. We needed more supplies: ointment and shampoo and bottles. Infant clothes needed laundering. There wasn't a place for the baby to sleep.

After saying goodbye to the kids, I'd inhaled in an attempt to flatten my protruding belly, needing at least two buttons of my coat to fasten. Giving up, I grabbed a scarf hanging on a hook near the front door and looped it around my neck to keep the Ukrainian winter air at bay. There were three weeks left until my due date. A simple pregnancy check-up coaxed me out the door with a promise of some much-needed time with my husband.

We'd sat in the car a few minutes, waiting for the engine to warm and for the frost to break up on the windshield. I could see my breath. "Let's swing by that American restaurant on the river after your appointment," Sergei suggested.

"You're on!" I said. "And I know what I am going to order: Eggs Benedict. I am going to eat it all, too. It's not like I can get any bigger than this, right?"

"You look beautiful," Sergei said.

At the appointment, I lay on a long brown bed and watched the obstetrician measure my stomach with the kind of measuring tape my mother used to make our clothes when we were kids. The doctor measured once.

"Hmm."

"Shto shto?" I asked in Russian. *What? What do you see? Is something wrong?*

Upon hearing my question, Sergei, who sat on the other side of the room, stood up and walked over to us.

"Shto takoye?" *Is there a problem?* Sergei asked.

"What? Oh no. Not a problem. I want to measure Gillian's belly one more time." The doctor positioned her right hand on the examination table next to my side and extended the tape across my abdomen. She hunched to ensure the right start and stop point on the tape and then held it out in front of her, stretching it wide.

"Your stomach hasn't grown in two weeks."

A sound like that of a police siren erupted inside my head, sending icy adrenaline shooting through me. *Our baby wasn't growing? Our baby wasn't growing.*

Sergei stood to the right of the doctor. He took hold of my hand and looked at me with that same steady gaze I'd noticed when we first met. When Sergei looked at a person, his eyes were unwavering, showing his confidence. At first that intimidated me but in our years together, it had become a great comfort. He heard what the doctor said and knew her words would worry me. He was *with me* and *present*, just as he'd been for the last seven years.

The baby had measured small at checkups earlier in my pregnancy but the doctor had never been concerned about it. At one point the baby measured three weeks behind her due date in size and development. At that time, the doctor reassured me that I had nothing to worry about. "She is growing which is the main thing," she'd said, winking. The doctor, jolly and round, acted like a female version of Kris Cringle. "There's no problem. Either we miscalculated the due date or you have a petite little girl in there," she'd explained as she turned her attention to Elaina and Zoya who happened to be with us at that appointment. "Now, girls, are you excited about the baby? And how do you like living in Ukraine?"

"Sergei, please tell her we are concerned." I'd wanted reassurance. To calm me, the doctor had ordered several ultrasounds and non-stress tests. Each time, the tests had shown the baby staying still. "Ona speet." *She's sleeping*, was all she'd say.

Today she said, "Here's what we are going to do, Gillian. We're going to admit you to the hospital overnight. I suspect the baby needs extra vitamins and nutrients. That should get her back on track."

"Should we worry? Is it something else?" I glared at Sergei the way wives do when they want their husbands to telepathically understand they should jump in with questions and concerns of their own.

"No! Don't worry!" the jolly doctor smiled at us.

Instead of heading off to breakfast as planned, we went directly to the hospital. By noon I sat gowned in a room on the fourth floor. A nurse hooked a monitor to my belly to follow the baby's heartbeats. I watched the squiggly green lines on the black screen dip low as my stomach tightened with each Braxton Hick's contraction. *Something is wrong. I know it.*

We were assigned a new doctor, tall and tan with a wide smile. His fuzzy, brown hair was gone in the back of his head. He wore glasses. He looked the part of the new Ukrainian, the guy who achieved success somehow during economic instability. The first two buttons of his crisp white shirt were open revealing a heavy chain that shimmered around his neck. Two huge, gold rings covered his knuckles. He was excited to have an American patient because he was learning English.

He introduced himself to Sergei first, in Russian, and shook hands with him. Then he peeked at me. "Hello, there. I see you having a baby? That's great. I…um…ugh… I am happy to be of assisting of you today here in Ukraine. I am fond of America. And, um…, I am tried to work on my English."

The new doctor continued to sputter and pause as he talked to me, searching for the right words to say in English. I would answer him in Russian, to let him know I could, and then wait for him to find his next English word.

I had studied Russian with a private tutor three times a week, two to three hours a session, for three and a half years. The day I met Tatiana Nikolayevna, my Russian teacher, I was nervous. She was a mountain of a woman with bleached blond hair. Her high cheekbones and pointed nose gave her a diplomatic air. She walked with a limp, suggesting she'd suffered a hip dislocation at some point in her life. One moment she'd give me an icy glare, then seconds later an approving smile would spread across her face.

For years I'd trudged along, immersing myself in basic conversation, memorization and grammar study. I cried at some point in every session. Tatiana was firm, but kind. In the beginning, I likened Russian to a blurry photograph. I knew something was there, but I could not make out the picture. It was humiliating and exhausting to try to speak a foreign language. Then one day the picture started to come into focus. I heard actual words, sentences, and eventually full conversations. I became an avid eavesdropper. My time deaf and mute in Ukraine came to an end. I had survived basic Russian language acquisition.

Outwardly I kept my cool at the hospital. But inside, I yelled at everyone who walked through the door. *Check me and go away! Let me lie here and worry in peace. I'm not in the mood to teach English as a second language.*

After meeting the new doctor and helping me settle into the room, Sergei left the hospital to go home and check on Elaina and Zoya and arrange the rest of the day's schedule. About an hour after he left, I realized I would need a few things to stay overnight. I called him on the cell but got voicemail. "Hi, it's me. Hope the kids are okay. Listen, since I'm going to be here for the night, can you grab a few things for me while you're home? I need a change of clothes, my contact case, and maybe a book to read. Thanks. Love you." After I hung up, I lay back on the hospital bed and focused on the clock on the opposite wall. There was nothing to do but wait. My hands were shaking.

Sergei got back to the hospital around four o'clock. Occasionally, the English-learning doctor came in, checked the monitor, and listened to my stomach with a stethoscope. Sergei asked questions. "How's the baby doing? Do we know if the glucose and extra vitamins are helping yet?" We discovered that one phrase the doctor knew well in both English and Russian was "wait and see." He would not outright answer our questions. "Wait and see," he'd say, already turning to leave.

By nine o'clock, our American colleagues started to call. Julie, the mother hen of our ex-pat group, called first. Her husband James was our team leader, and they had been living in Ukraine for over ten years.

"I hope you don't mind, but I called Lydia to tell her about you and the baby." Lydia was another American working with us. Before moving to Ukraine, she was a postnatal nurse at Children's Memorial Hospital in Chicago.

"That's fine, Julie," I muttered, my frustration breaking through. I wasn't mad at Julie. I was mad that I was stuck in the hospital. I was mad that we were told over and over again to wait and see.

Julie continued, "And we are coming to the hospital. Once our sitter gets here, James and I will pick up Lydia and we'll be on our way."

As soon as I hung up, the phone rang again. Lydia's voice, strong but soft, filled my ear with questions and greetings.

The threat of tears tightened my throat and I could only manage a whisper, "The baby hasn't grown at all since the last visit to the doctor two weeks ago. I have an IV in right now, and I'm receiving glucose and other vitamins. The doctor says this will help bulk the baby up and get her back on track." Sergei sat in the corner of the hospital room, pretending to be interested in a newspaper he'd picked up in the hospital lobby.

"Whenever I feel a contraction, the green squiggly line on the monitor drops low," I said. I expected a response from Lydia. Instead, silence. For a second, I wondered if the phone lost its connection.

"Gillian, I will be there in a half hour. The next time your doctor comes in the room, you need to demand an emergency c-section. I don't want to scare you, but in the States your baby would have already been delivered. She is not doing well. She's in trouble. Listen to me; you have to talk to your doctor." I tightened my grip on the phone. Sergei stood up, came over and sat down on my bed. "What's wrong?" he mouthed. I shook my head and turned to the window.

"Okay, Lydia. We'll tell him." I hung up the phone and started to cry. Sergei leaned in and took me in his arms.

"Lydia said it sounds like the baby is in extreme distress. She said we need to demand a c-section."

Always pragmatic, Sergei wondered out loud, "How can we know she is right? She isn't even here. The doctor said the baby needs some extra help." I moved out of Sergei's arms so I could look him in the eye.

"Lydia said if we were in the States, the baby would have already been delivered." I felt a sob rise and my body began shaking. "Sergei, please find the doctor."

My husband agreed and went to get the doctor. I was alone. *I knew it. I'd known for weeks that something was wrong. I should have spoken up more. Oh God, please let the baby live. I want to go home.* I did not trust the doctors in this hospital. I wanted my mother. A few minutes later, Sergei came back to the room with the English-learning doctor who had his usual broad smile.

"Umm, your husband said that you are worried that the baby be born?"

"Yes. I have an American friend who is a nurse. I talked to her on the phone and she said that with the baby's heart beat dropping so low, I would have already had a caesarean section if we were in the States. I'm worried. We need to talk about delivering the baby."

I stared at this man who was dressed in white pants and a white, button-down shirt with a lazy stethoscope draped around his neck. He was a doctor. I wasn't sure of the schooling process in Ukraine, but in America he would have completed close to a decade of education in order to qualify for this job. *Shouldn't he know? Didn't he know?*

"The baby is stabilizing with the IV. It hasn't been enough time. I think we should wait and see. She needs more time." The doctor glanced from my face and Sergei's to see if his words registered. Sergei spouted back in Russian.

They talked a few more minutes and then the doctor smiled at both of us and left. The clock next to my hospital bed read eleven o'clock at night. The baby had been receiving fluids since noon. I studied the monitor next to my head. The baby's heart rate still dropped once in a while.

"He doesn't know what he's doing!" I snapped at Sergei.

"I know this is hard, but he's a doctor. He's *your* doctor. We should listen to him. And I'm not saying this lightly. That's my baby too in there. I'm worried. But Lydia isn't here and the doctor is, and I think we should listen to him."

Julie, James and Lydia arrived within the hour. They were upbeat, commenting on the nice hospital room, cracking jokes and squinting at me through the room's bright lights. All three tried to act like it was the most natural thing in the world to hang out in a Ukrainian hospital room at midnight. I loved them for it.

A nurse located the English-learning doctor. When he came into the room, Lydia stepped forward and introduced herself. She went on to tell him what she told me on the phone. As she spoke, she kept taking steps closer to him. Soon, she stood right in front of his face. The doctor no longer smiled. "Doctor, this baby needs a cesarean section right away!" James and Julie hung back on the other side of the room. Sergei got up from the bed and stood next to Lydia.

"We are going to wait and see if the IV helps," the doctor declared. Lydia persisted, eyeing my husband for language assistance and nodding incessantly as her words poured in a mixture of English and Russian. Her stern face and tone of voice pleaded with the doctor to take action.

I could tell by the projection of her voice that Lydia meant business. Here was one of my people, not only a colleague and a friend, but an American medical professional weighing in on the fate of my child.

After hearing more from Lydia, Sergei took her side. "We need to see if anything else is going on with the baby. My wife is frightened. We don't want to wait and see anymore." Sergei squared his deep blue eyes on the doctor.

"All right. I guess we can take a closer look at the baby through an ultrasound."

"Spaseebo," Sergei said. *Thank you.* "Spaseebo," Julie, James, and Lydia all chimed in.

"Nyezashto," the doctor replied. *Don't mention it.* His expression was blank when he left the room.

Twenty minutes later I concentrated on Sergei's face, as a coiled cord smeared icy liquid over my midsection. Doctors and nurses huddled around the ultrasound screen, whispering to one another in Russian. The technician tapped on my stretched skin, seeking the baby's beating heart beneath it. As my abdomen tightened again, the small huddle of Ukrainian professionals all gasped at the monitor.

"Sergei, ask them what they see."

Sergei cleared his throat. "Izveneete pozshalusta. Shto takoye?" *Excuse me, please. What is wrong?* Our doctor turned around from the group and faced us. *Oh no, here we go.* Sergei took my hand in his.

"The baby's heart beat goes too low with the contractions. We need to do a caesarean section right away."

Back in my room, shaved and ready for surgery, I perched on the end of the high hospital bed and studied the imperfections on the tan walls. Sergei had gone downstairs to sign papers to allow the surgery. James, Julie and Lydia had gone to search for the nearest waiting room. All of a sudden I felt the need to take everything in. I wanted to remember every detail. A well-polished wooden desk with a matching chair stood against the wall in front of me. Cream-colored curtains with deep pleats framed the window. My stocking feet dangled above the alabaster tile floor. They seemed disconnected from my body.

I thought about Elaina and Zoya sleeping in their Estonian-made bunk beds back at the apartment. Sergei and I searched all over Kiev before purchasing the pale, hardwood beds. Thick cotton blankets were probably tucked up under the girls' chins.

I imagined their *Babushka*, Sergei's mother, asleep in the next room, ready to provide a drink of water or a trip to the toilet. I wished I had kissed them goodnight.

I heard footsteps in the hall. The doctor stuck his head through the doorway. "Gotova?" No time for English now.

I nodded—*ready*.

Two orderlies were at my side helping me from the high hospital bed onto a cold gurney with a starchy white sheet. *Sergei? What is taking you so long?* They wheeled my gurney down the hall. I looked to my right and to my left for my husband. "Sergei!" I cried out.

"I'm here. I'm here." Sergei, suddenly at my side, covered my hands with his. "God, please protect our baby and give Gillian peace." He lifted his eyes to mine and smiled, almost giddy, "She's coming tonight!"

I could not believe his exuberance. I was headed off to battle for our child, while he would sit in a waiting room and leaf through a magazine. Julie, James and Lydia waved at me from the waiting area. "I want to get a good picture of the three of you after the baby comes," Julie called out.

Sergei squeezed my hand and gave me a quick kiss as the orderlies whisked me through thick, metal double doors. The temperature dropped. Nurses and doctors buzzed around the room. Russian words spun above my head, but I couldn't understand a thing. Their voices were drowned out by my chattering teeth. When we chose this private hospital they had asked if I'd like to have an interpreter for the birth. Assuming Sergei would help, I'd said no. Now it was two o'clock in the morning and no spoken words made sense. I was alone, lying on a gurney in a surgical room in the former Soviet Union.

The English-learning doctor prepared his instruments. The anesthesiologist greeted me, "Dobriy vecher. Ya budu delat vam ukol v speenu." Simple words in Russian. *Good evening, I am going to place this needle here in your back.* She must have seen the confusion on my face because she helped me sit up and started to pantomime the needle going into my spine. Her face was close to mine and her breath reeked of cigarette smoke. *What am I doing here? Why did we decide to save money and have the baby in Ukraine instead of going back to the States? I was too flippant in the planning.* "It's our third," I'd said to Sergei. "What can go wrong?"

The room was the kind of frigid you feel when you sit outside on a cement bench in the dead of winter. Ukrainians have a superstition about women sitting on cold cement. When we moved to Kiev three and a half years earlier, I had rested on a cement block outside a grocery store waiting for Sergei. An old woman came up to me and pointed her finger in my face. Her voice raised a few decibels with each word. She kept waving her hands up and down until I understood what she wanted me to do. I stood up. "People believe if a woman sits on cold cement too long she will become infertile," Sergei explained to me later when I told him about the heckling. Perhaps the old woman had been right. Though I was not infertile, the baby inside me was in some kind of trouble.

On the operating table, I felt a stinging prick in my lower back, smack dab in the middle of my spine. It was not my first epidural. I'd had one for Elaina's birth five years before in the States.

Her birth had been controlled, almost easy. After settling in my room at the hospital they had administered the epidural, instantly removing the throbbing pain of the contractions. There was nothing else to do but wait to push. Sergei and I cracked jokes and phoned family and friends to tell them we were in labor. The most dramatic thing about Elaina's birth was me yelling at Sergei to slow down on the way to the hospital at 2 o'clock in the morning. "Do you have to hit every pot hole in the street?" I'd complained while we raced towards the hospital in our rusted-out Chevy.

It was now 2 o'clock in the morning once again and time to give birth. Warmth spread through my belly and down to my toes because of the epidural. A nurse laid me back on the hospital table. I thought my c-section would be like those television shows you see in the States: the little curtain at the woman's midsection, the husband seated by the wife's head, the baby's cry filling the room as the doctor lifts up the child to proclaim, "It's a girl!" Instead a nurse placed a mask over my mouth and nose. *They were putting me to sleep? No one bothered to tell me about general anesthesia?* My body and my baby would be in the hands of the Ukrainian delivery doctor who wanted to practice his English.

I concentrated on the low, buzzing white ceiling. The anesthesiologist appeared in my line of vision. "Count backwards from ten," she commanded. Her lips were painted a frothy pink, reminding me of a dab of cotton candy that evaporates in your mouth.

Count in English or Russian? The hum of the fluorescent lights now started to overwhelm. *And why wasn't the anesthesiologist wearing a mask? I wasn't supposed to know she wore lipstick. Was I?* "Desyat, devyat, vosem," my voice shook as I managed to count backwards from ten to one in Russian, "sem ..." I started to feel myself drift, away from the doctor—a scowl now on his face as he bent over my abdomen. I floated away from the anesthesiologist waiting for her next smoke break, away from my friends keeping Sergei company in the lobby, away from the little one struggling in my womb. I floated upwards towards a bright, yellow light.

3

A nurse was putting away supplies on the other side of the room when I woke up the morning after the surgery. She was blurry. I blinked a few times before realizing a cloudy partition stood between us. She walked over to my bed. "Kak vy sebya chust-vuyute," she asked. *How do you feel?* She was a petite young woman, her plain dark hair pulled back in a ponytail. I thought about the nurses I'd had in the States the two other times I had given birth. They were friendly and talkative. After Zoya's birth, I wanted a few bored nurses to leave me alone. I had been the only mom on the floor and they hung around the room all day, smiling and fussing over us.

"Harasho," I answered in Russian. *I feel fine.* "Where's my baby?"

"Your husband will explain everything to you when he gets here. For now, you should sleep," the nurse said, already walking away from me.

Eight months earlier, our family vacationed at our *hata*, a summer home we'd purchased with our friends Jim and Liz. By then, we had been living in Ukraine over two years.

A Ukrainian summer home is not what I had imagined. I remember the first time a friend in Kiev told me about her place in the village.

"What are you doing this weekend, Oksana?" I'd asked at an evening get-together.

"I will be in the village with my mother at our summer home."

"Oh wow. That sounds great to get away from the city and relax."

"No, you do not understand. We do not go there to relax. We go to the village to dig potatoes and to work in the garden. We must get enough vegetables for our family to eat for now, to have for later, and to sell in the marketplace."

The house and land in the village cost four hundred American dollars. We had split the cost of the hata with our friends, thus securing a rustic get-away for a couple hundred bucks and the price of an air mattress.

The house had two rooms—one large and one small— and an enclosed porch. It sat in a valley, hidden by a steep hill on one side and thick, green woods around the rest of the property. There was no heat, running water or cell phone service. The bathroom was a detached shack out back—a deep hole dug out, wood slabs, and a white plastic toilet seat. With no roof on the outhouse, you could look up at the stars.

Our little family was tucked away from everything that week. Our vacation plan was to stay as long as the meat didn't spoil. No one could reach us at the *hata*. I joked with Sergei that if it were the end of the world, we wouldn't have known for a couple of days. We needed that kind of get-away; the four of us, a blazing sun, and hours spread out.

The village, two hours from Kiev, cozied up to the Dnieper River, one of Europe's largest waterways, flowing from Russia through Belarus and down into the Black Sea. It was a filthy river, with talk of residual pollution from the infamous 1986 Chernobyl power plant explosion, sixty miles north of Kiev. Elaina and Zoya weren't allowed to swim in the river, but a relatively clean pond hidden in the village would suffice.

Our first morning at the *hata*, the girls rolled out of bed and started playing outside in their pajamas. The weather was perfect for idleness; we sunned ourselves at the pond all afternoon and enjoyed a picnic of vegetables, bread, and thick slices of sausage and cheese. The girls reminded me of long-legged spiders, crawling over the sand as fast as they could, scattering around as if the rock they'd been hiding under had been flipped. By the time the sun peaked, Elaina and Zoya were bronze from head to toe, their hair sun-kissed white.

Later that day, after supper, we walked up to the only store in the village. It mostly stocked assorted brands of vodka and beer, as well as sausage, bread and ice cream. We purchased four sticks of vanilla covered in chocolate and started towards home, kicking stones and letting the ice cream drip down our chins. A goat meandered ahead of us on the dirt road. Chickens squawked and pecked at one another off to the side. The sun dipped to the horizon.

Sergei picked up Zoya and put her on his shoulders. I watched my daughter, three years old, and was struck by her serenity. *Zoya* is the Ukrainian version of the Greek name Zoe, meaning *new life*. I had been a panicked, shaky new mother with Elaina. Eighteen months later, Zoya's arrival settled me down. She ate and slept when she wanted, and she was happiest near me. Because of her calm and trust, Zoya eased me.

Elaina walked by my side, pouting, wanting a turn on Papa's shoulders. Her name means *light*, but a better definition for her is *lightning*. She came out of the womb keen and quick, and aced each new skill in her young life. I took her small hand in mine, this little girl who could light up a room. My daughters were opposites. The yin and yang that balanced my life. I sucked in a breath while one of the goats ahead of me bleated. The girls were so beautiful; I couldn't help but marvel at them and the evolution of our family.

Sergei and I met in Ukraine in 1996. Six years after the Cold War ended, government officials opened Russia, Ukraine and other Slavic countries to religious and philanthropic organizations to help them rebuild. I was twenty years old and had taken a year off from college to work in the schools and universities in Kiev. Sergei interpreted for our group. At first, I'd found his country harsh and cold, but by the end of that year, I had fallen in love with him and Ukraine. He followed me back to the United States after I returned home.

Having lived in Ukraine for over two years as a family, we were starting to feel settled. I had finished intensive language acquisition. Elaina loved her preschool and Sergei was part of a new church plant in the neighborhood where he grew up. Zoya started to respond to us in Russian and I felt less and less exhausted at the end of long, Ukrainian days. I secretly thought of myself as both an architect and a builder. We had put down the scaffolding needed to function well as a mostly-American family in Ukraine. My life was going as planned. Our family lived and worked in Ukraine and we were thriving.

Before our vacation to the *hata*, Sergei and I had kicked around the idea of having another child. The timing seemed right. If I sat still and quiet, I could feel a gentle tug to continue to build our family. I wanted another baby. I wanted more of this.

As we walked home from the village store, I squeezed Elaina's hand one, two, three times and pointed out a cow grazing down below the dirt road in a meadow. She forgot about her pouting. "Wow, look at that cow! Papa, do you see the cow? Look Zo Zo, cow!" Yes, I wanted another child, and the *hata* was the perfect setting to pursue that goal.

That night, after spending the day at the pond and buying ice cream, and after the girls were tucked away inside, fast asleep, I climbed on top of my husband as he sat in a folding chair next to the crackling bonfire. It was probably close to midnight. A cool August breeze swept the hair on my forearms up. The glass of Chardonnay I'd sipped at dinner helped me change gears from mother to wife.

"No one is around," I whispered in Sergei's ear.

The nearest neighbor was up a steep hill. The road was quiet. Crickets called to one another in the woods surrounding our property.

I peeled off my gray sweatshirt and leaned into Sergei's neck. He smelled like earth and oak and chocolate. I sensed a faint smile on his lips. I would have been embarrassed if some-one knew I was making love to my husband, who was also the pastor of our church, in a folding chair under a black night. I mean, we were missionaries. But the darkness enveloped us.

Sergei reached into his pocket for a condom.

"No. We don't need it."

"You sure? You want to try for another baby?" he hesi-tated.

"Yes, let's," I said, covering his mouth with mine. The sky housed a thousand stars.

An hour later, I sank into my sleeping bag on the air mattress Sergei bought for our reprieve in the village, but I couldn't sleep.

"I think we just made a baby," I whispered to Sergei. Envious of how fast he fell asleep, I lay there into the night, tucked in my royal blue sleeping bag two hours from our apartment in Kiev, an ocean away from where I slept as a child in Michigan.

I'm ready for this, right?

Sergei showed up at the hospital around eight o'clock that morning, about an hour and a half after I had woken up from the surgery. Unshaven, wearing the same clothes from the previous day, he bent and kissed me like I had seen him kiss his mother countless times. Just a slight brush of the lips. Taking a closer look at his face, I noticed his eyes were puffy. *What is going on? Had he been crying?*

"How are you feeling?" he asked, standing over me, concerned.

"I'm sore. I still can't feel my legs from the epidural." I peered down at the sheets covering my motionless legs. "Sergei, where's our baby?"

"She's on another floor in an incubator," he said. "She was in a bad shape when they took her from you." Though a native Russian speaker, my husband's English is excellent. If he makes a mistake, he is either tired or nervous.

"She was all shriveled up, and she wasn't breathing when she came out. The doctor resuscitated her. She has some kind of blood infection too."

I tried to focus on his words, but the black circles underneath Sergei's eyes kept distracting me. He and his mom both get dark circles under their eyes when they are tired. It happens often. I am used to seeing my husband with raccoon eyes. He's busy. His time is spent caring for people. I had never seen the skin under his eyes so black.

I glanced away. A light rain splattered drop after indifferent drop on the window by my bed. I was quite taken with the tiny, perfect bodies of water. They'd freefall and then break open and slide down the pane. I tried to comprehend what Sergei had just said: not breathing when born, blood infection, all shriveled up. *He can't be talking about our baby. The day we conceived this child the sun beat down on us. The night when we came together was beautiful and clear. How could her first day out of my womb be this dark and wet?*

There were people outside of the hospital getting out of the shower, having coffee, leaving their apartments for work.

"The doctor said she wouldn't have made it 'til morning. At this point they're still not sure if she will make it today." Sergei looked past me. "I have something else to tell you."

My body tensed.

"They suspect the baby may have Down syndrome. They sent her blood work off for testing this morning. The head pediatrician is coming to talk to us at nine o'clock."

After Sergei spoke those words, I stared past him. I felt nothing. Even now, years later, when I recall that moment; the very first time the words *Down syndrome* were uttered, the memory is barren.

Then my mind found its way back to Jamie Hanson, a girl with Down syndrome I knew in high school. At first, I was afraid of her. Her tongue seemed too big for her mouth, and she smiled and giggled a lot. Jamie was my age but she was still like a child. She hung out with our high school group at church before class started and then went to her Sunday school class with the third graders. All the kids in our group hugged and fussed over her; I ignored my aversion in order to fit in, but I knew in my heart that I was pretending.

I saw Jamie with her mom one time at the grocery store while I was home visiting my parents, a year or two after I graduated from high school and moved to Chicago for college. Mrs. Hanson clipped through the produce section, while Jamie shuffled behind her with her head down. She kept tripping over her feet. I had graduated and moved on to college. Perhaps Jamie still attended the third grade Sunday school class at church. Having an adult child wasn't fair. Being a kid in a woman's body complete with breasts and a menstrual cycle didn't seem fair either.

Sergei let go of my hand and went to put his bag in the chair in the corner of the room. He came and sat next to me on the bed. "I saw the girls this morning before I left for the hospital." *Had he been talking this whole time?* I focused back on his face. "They're excited about the baby. They said to give you a kiss from them. I decided to wait to tell them about the baby once we know more. My mom is there with them, and Lena will come back later today to give her a break. Gillian?"

I tried to listen. *She can't have Down syndrome, can she? The doctors are mistaken. Or maybe this is like Zoya's birth?*

When Zoya was born in Michigan, a nurse thought she might have Down syndrome. While I slept, she checked the baby's hands for the simian crease, a straight line that runs across the palm, fairly common in children with Down syndrome. She examined Zoya's low set eyes for slanting. Later that day Sergei came to the hospital with Elaina to visit us. The nurse told us that she laughed when she saw them. Zoya didn't have Down syndrome. She was Slavic! Her eyes were low set and farther apart like Sergei's. She looked like her Papa.

Was this the case again? Although, this was Ukraine, and the staff must have noticed something other than Ukrainian facial features. Sergei's hand trembled as he handed me a few pieces of paper. "When I got home this morning, I went online and tried to find information about Down syndrome. I only had a little bit of time, but I did find a few things." He pushed the crinkled printouts under my nose. One page read "Myths and Truths about Down syndrome." I skimmed through the text:

> **Myth:** Down syndrome is a rare genetic disorder.

> **Truth:** Down syndrome is the most commonly occurring genetic condition. One in every 800 live births is a child with Down syndrome. Today, more than 350,000 people in the United States have Down syndrome.

I stared at the information. *Down syndrome is a commonly occurring genetic condition?* My mind tried to grasp what I read. Genetic meant that if my baby had Down syndrome, maybe she'd gotten it from Sergei or me.

> **Myth:** Most children with Down syndrome are born to older parents.

> **Truth:** Most children with Down syndrome are born to women younger than 35 years old simply because younger women have more children. However, the incidence of births of children with Down syndrome increases with the age of the mother.

I had turned 31 years old the previous month.

Myth: People with Down syndrome are severely "retarded."

Truth: Most people with Down syndrome have IQs that fall in the mild to moderate range of intellectual disability (formerly known as "retardation"). Children with Down syndrome fully participate in public and private educational programs.

There was the word I was trying not to call to mind: *retarded.* If my baby had Down syndrome it meant she was retarded. *I might have a stupid baby.* I blinked back tears and squinted up from the page to Sergei. He stood next to me. His head cocked to the side, he looked at me out of the corners of his eyes. I'd come to know that when Sergei spied like that, he was deep in thought. *Is he thinking our baby is retarded?* I read on.

Myth: Most people with Down syndrome are institutionalized.

Truth: Today people with Down syndrome live at home with their families and are active participants in the educational, vocational, social, and recreational activities of the community. They are integrated into the regular education system and take part in sports, camping, music, art programs and all the other activities of their communities. People with Down syndrome are valued members of their families and their communities, contributing to society in a variety of ways.

Sure, in America people with Down syndrome are valued, but what about in Ukraine? This information is from the United States. The previous spring, I'd seen a man with Down syndrome taking a walk with his father in our neighborhood, well before the thought of having another child even occurred to me. He ambled alongside his dad. He looked about forty. His father, a senior citizen, reminded me of a yellowed photograph torn around the edges, developed and stored away before acid free paper was invented. They eased forward together.

At first, I was envious of their peaceful pace. My kids ran ahead of me, screaming and laughing and jumping into soppy puddles of melted snow. But then I was sorry for them. Up until that point I hadn't seen anyone in Kiev with mental disabilities. Both father and son seemed tired and sad. The snow was almost all gone, revealing dirty yards and muddy, gray sidewalks. How many walks had this father and son taken together in their lifetime? How many times had they witnessed the snow fall and then months later, walked through the dirty streets as the temperature rose in preparation for spring?

"How many people have you seen in Kiev with Down syndrome or some other type of obvious disability?" I asked Sergei later that day after telling him about the sad father and son we saw out on our walk.

"You know, I don't recall seeing anyone like that in the city, not counting war veterans who lost limbs."

"How can that be? There have to be families with kids who are handicapped," I had challenged with Western indignation.

I held this overpowering opinion that my country was better than Sergei's.

"Simple. A lot of pregnant women get an amniocentesis. If there is a disability, they abort. Or, if a child is born in the hospital with something like Down syndrome, it's not uncommon for the parents to forfeit their parenting rights and leave the hospital empty-handed. And if people *do* take their babies home, they probably keep them hidden from the rest of the world, or send them off to a village to live with relatives."

I pushed the myths and truths page to the side. The next page was an article written by a woman whose granddaughter had Down syndrome. As I read her story, I thought about my parents back in the States. With the arrival of this baby, they now had a total of eight grandchildren. They were halfway around the world, seven hours behind us in time, both fast asleep in bed. I imagined my father's snoring filling up the house, like it did in my childhood. How would I tell my parents? And my sister Amy? My brother Justin? I imagined the news breaking out in my small town. *Poor Gillian. Her life seemed so great, happily married with two adorable little girls. She was doing important work in Ukraine and now this: a retarded baby. It's so sad.*

Sergei waited for me to finish reading. I peeked up at him. Part of me wanted to be held. I needed to cry in his arms. But I could not let myself break down because that meant conceding. I turned my head back to the window. Although he stood in front of me, it felt like Sergei left.

I held still and focused on the raindrops.

5

The first time I'd felt the baby move, I was in the bath, looking down at my cushiony middle. The movement was just a flutter. The baby probably wasn't much bigger than the palm of my hand. I loved taking baths, and when I got pregnant I continued my nightly ritual. The tub was deep and wide. The warm water swirled, while soap bubbles popped and fizzled around me. I would lay in the bath and commune with my unborn child. It was us against the world, protected by the high, Pepto Bismol-colored walls of the tub. I was happy, regardless of loneliness or homesickness or frustration over the Russian language.

Around the time I first felt the baby move, Sergei brought home a few books for me to read. Once in a while he'd stumble across a vendor who sold books in English at an outdoor market in Kiev. Whenever he'd come home with something new, it was like Christmas morning. One book in the pile caught my eye. *Jewel* by Bret Lott. The story took place in the backwoods of Mississippi in the 1940s. Based on true events, it was about a woman whose sixth child, Brenda Kay, was born with Down syndrome. I read the book in one sitting, ignoring my husband and kids.

The day I finished the book, I was sitting on the bed in our room. The sun was setting. The children were already in bed, even though it wasn't dark yet. The air was tinted green. I thought about my baby growing inside me.

"I couldn't do it," I told Sergei. "I could never mother a child like Brenda Kay."

A group of Ukrainian doctors paraded into my hospital room at nine o'clock sharp. I wondered if a team approach was how it was done in Ukrainian upscale hospitals. But then I remembered; they were here because our child was struggling.

The head pediatrician looked more like a rock star than a doctor. Her shoulder length hair was brassy blond, highlighted with multiple shades of red. Her makeup was thick: deep blue eye shadow, bright pink blush and red lipstick. She seemed official in spite of the makeup, with a clipboard in her hand and the trademark stethoscope around her neck. A crisp, white medical coat covered her bright and stylish clothes. Her colleague had dark brown hair that hung limply to her shoulders. She wore no makeup. A large mole with long gray hairs growing out of its center sat above her lip. Neither woman smiled. The Rock Star addressed Sergei in Russian.

"Right now the baby is in an incubator. She cannot keep up her body temperature. It's hard for her to breathe on her own. Your daughter has low blood platelets. She has an infection in her blood that we are trying to fix through an infusion. She's jaundiced, too. It is too soon to know if the baby will even make it. We are doing everything we can."

I did not care for the doctor's bedside manner. She came across as noncommittal, "Look, I can't promise anything, so don't blame me if something goes wrong." Her tone seemed to apologize for what she could not do for our child.

I stopped listening, a trick much easier to do with a foreign language. There was something about the sound of her voice and the way she looked at us that felt like pity. I didn't want her pity. "You were dealt a bad hand. We'll just have to wait and see how this all plays out," I imagined she'd say if she could. At that moment, I hated her.

Elaina was jaundiced as a newborn. The first few days home from the hospital I sat outside with her on our spacious Chicago porch so the sun could boost her vitamin D production. I was traumatized that there was something wrong with my newborn and couldn't believe it would be corrected with natural light. But after two hours in the sun, her orange skin started to pink up. A few days later at the pediatrician's office her bilirubin levels were perfect.

While my mind was wandering back to Chicago, wishing I could make my baby better with something as simple as sitting in the sun, I realized the doctor was still talking. Russian words were cutting the air with guttural noises and sharp consonants. The medical team looked pensive and solemn. I heard the words *seendrom dauna*.

Sergei stood next to my hospital bed. He paid attention to the doctor, although the information wasn't new to him. I wished he and I were alone.

I glanced over to the side table next to my bed. There sat a tan telephone, a plastic cup filled with water, a straw and three pages of information about Down syndrome. A vial of the baby's blood had already been sent off to a geneticist for testing.

I understood the doctor's final sentence. "We will get the test results soon and then, depending on what they are, you can decide what you are going to do with the baby."

6

The nursery had a plain gray door and behind it was a room where my baby lay. This would be the first time I'd see her. I was in a wheelchair, still too weak from the surgery to make the journey on foot.

We had made our way through the halls. Now we stopped at the door, and I looked up at Sergei needing some of his confidence. He turned the knob, then slowly pushed my wheelchair through the doorway.

In the corner of the room stood a lone incubator.

Sergei wheeled me to it. "There she is," he said softly. "There's our baby." He took a few steps back from the plexiglass dome to give me space. I reached through the small window and laid my hand on her chest.

"Hi, Little One, I'm your mommy," I whispered. I needed to hear those words out loud, because I didn't quite believe them.

"What do you think?" Sergei asked, stepping up behind me. He put his hand on my shoulder. The warmth of his palm penetrated through my hospital gown.

The baby's eyes were shut tight, her little chest worked hard to contract with every breath. I leaned in, my mid-section throbbing, and studied her face. Her lips were cracked. Both her ankles were peeling and she had long toes. I had no words.

When I was a kid, I used to watch *Mork and Mindy*, Robin Williams' quirky show about an alien who comes to earth in an egg and falls in love with a beautiful human. During the theme song in the beginning of the show, Mork and Mindy are clinging to opposing goal posts on a football field. They are waving their arms, trying to get the other to come to their side but it's no use. It was such a clever beginning, a metaphor of their relationship. *A relationship between an alien and a human cannot work.* I swallowed hard, feeling the impossibility of ever connecting with this child if she turned out to have a condition I did not really understand.

Sergei stooped to examine the baby. "I feel bad that she is stuck in there and we don't get to hold her." He crouched a bit more so his face was up against hers behind the plastic.

"Doesn't her hair remind you of Elaina's?"

I nodded. She did have a full head of golden hair like Elaina's when she was born. "It's the same color, blond but with a touch of red, and, look, she is long like Elaina was too," my voice wavered. "Sergei, can you see it? Can you see Down syndrome?"

"I don't know. I go back and forth. Her eyes do slant. But they've hardly been open so it's hard to know for sure. Besides, her birth was traumatic. Even though she is littler than the others, I think she looks a lot like Elaina and Zoya. She looks like a Marchenko."

I considered Sergei's words. *She looks like a Marchenko.* I expected her to look like she had Down syndrome.

Beep, beep, beep, the black screen with the squiggly green line kept announcing that our daughter was living, even if it was in a lonely incubator. My stomach started to turn and I needed to lie down.

"You ready to go?" Sergei asked.

I stroked the baby's chest and nodded.

7

My mother walked into my hospital room wearing a yellow rain-
coat with red, blue and purple polka dots. Coral lipstick had been
applied to both her lips and her cheeks, like she had always done
while I was growing up. I was back from seeing our baby for the
first time. When she came in, I started to cry.

"Look at you, Mom. Aren't you brave?" I said in a small
voice. Even though we had all decided that my mother would
make the trip to Ukraine when the time was right, I was amazed
she had made the long journey alone, and now she was here.

Just a week prior, in preparation for her arrival, I had spent
five hours lugging my huge belly around Kiev searching for
American-sized washcloths. "Gillian, what are you doing? Your
mom doesn't care if we have washcloths or not." "Sergei, my
mom takes baths every night, and she likes to wash with a wash-
cloth." None of my family from the States had seen our lives in
Ukraine. I wanted my mom to like it and to see that we were
happy. I wanted her to see that we weren't going without things.
I found washcloths in the very last store, in a new part of town,
and purchased four fluffy white ones before climbing the final
bus towards home.

Hugging her now felt so good. It reminded me of when I
was a little girl and she was the one in the hospital. When I was
five years old, my mom had a hysterectomy. A doctor removed
parts of her that had once housed my brother, sister, and me.
I remember having no idea why she was there. No one had
explained anything.

"She needed an operation," my father offered, tight lipped, as he placed a grilled cheese sandwich and a glass of milk in front of me.

Life's rhythm was off. I ate burnt scrambled eggs for breakfast. I wore the same clothes every day. My brother and sister fought more. "Dad, Justin hit me!" "She started it!" My father didn't tuck me in at bedtime. At night I ached for my mom. In child time, she was gone for years. In real time, it was about two weeks. My dad took Justin, Amy, and me to see her in the hospital. When we got inside, I gripped my dad's hand. The iridescent lights hurt my eyes and made the gurneys lined up in the hallway glimmer. The white walls seemed like a maze. It was the early 80s, and kids weren't allowed to visit patients in the hospital. My dad deposited us in a room with rows of mauve chairs and plastic ferns and told us to wait while he went to say hi to our mom. Justin and Amy argued over who was in charge. I watched them bicker. I was scared.

After a little while, my dad came back to the waiting room with a strange woman. Her bleached hair stuck up all over. She wore a light blue housecoat and pulled a silver coat rack alongside her. The woman's skin looked like dried up Elmer's glue. I smelled cigarettes.

My dad bent down. Our eyes locked. "Gilly, this is Mrs. Shultz. She's going to take you to see mom. Her room is down the hallway."

The woman smiled. *Mrs. Shultz?* Not a doctor or a nurse. She had a tube coming out of her arm. *My father expected me to go away with a stranger in a housecoat?*

"Hi there, little girl. Scoot on in here under my robe. I'll take you to see your mama." Mrs. Shultz opened her housecoat.

Her pajamas were brown and threadbare. I glared at my dad. He nodded, prodding me to obey. I craved my mom, but I didn't want to go anywhere with this woman. Timid, I stuck a foot out and forced my body to follow suit. One step landed me next to Mrs. Shultz. I came up to the middle of her thigh. "That's it. Now I'm going to button up my housecoat. Be real quiet now."

Mrs. Shultz's body heat emanated through her thin pajamas. I started to sweat. I wasn't even supposed to talk to strangers and now I was hiding in some lady's housecoat. Inside, all I saw was a haze of light blue. Closing my eyes I willed myself not to cry. My dad was already shouting at the others. "Justin, stop touching her! Sit down!"

"All righty, let's go!" Mrs. Shultz crooned. She took a step, suddenly four legs instead of two. I stuck with her, my hands down at my sides, and held my breath. We toddled down the hallway, unnoticed.

"Annie, we've got a visitor!" Mrs. Shultz yelled. We veered right and trudged through a door. *Annie? My mom?* Maybe Mrs. Shultz *was* taking me to see my mom. I was frightened. *Was she whole? The mother I knew? Perhaps surgery meant she no longer would be herself.* I wanted to stay in the housecoat.

Mrs. Shultz unbuttoned us. My eyes were closed tight. I opened them and saw my mother. She was sitting on a hospital bed. Her dark hair hung down around her shoulders. She looked normal, like the mother I knew. I rushed over and clung to her. She had on her soft pink nightgown, the one I loved so much, with little embroidered roses. In my mother's arms, I started to cry.

She held me close and whispered into my hair, "I'm so glad to see you, Gilly. I missed you," I was held back, examined.

"How are you? Were you scared with Mrs. Shultz?" "I'm okay, mom," I answered.

My mom's arms then loosened, relaxed. And I had a moment of childhood awakening. It dawned on me that her life rhythm had been off as well. She needed me like I needed her. This was the bliss of reciprocated comfort, something I would later dream about when I thought of becoming a mother.

Now we were hugging in another hospital room, a world away from the first one. I thought about the baby across the hall, who I hadn't even held yet. I tightened my grip on my mom.

After four days, the pink card on our baby's incubator still did not have a name written on it. That morning, the doctor on rounds had told me, "If you do well today, you can go home tomorrow." I could stay longer, because my stay was paid for up front, but I could also go home and leave our yet-unnamed baby if I wanted. The hospital would stand in my place as a caregiver.

Outside my window, a lifeless tree stood. The branches on the bottom were wide, sturdy. They grew more narrow and brittle as they went higher. At the tip of the tree sat a blackbird. He was there every day, all day. He could fly. I had seen him come and land once, first thing in the morning right before I'd gotten out of bed, but day after day he stayed put. I couldn't help feeling like the presence of the bird was urging me to stay, even though everything inside me wanted to flee.

We had no genetic test results yet, but while a nurse was changing my sheets, she said off-handedly, "That's what you get for assuming you could have three normal children." Ukrainians usually have one child per family; in wanting this child, I had asked for too much.

Five days. The name card stood empty.

I had happily picked Elaina and Zoya's names. Elaina was named after my grandmother Elaine, and Zoya was chosen out of a Ukrainian baby book Sergei's mom had mailed to us.

"Sergei, it's your turn to choose," I declared. "I picked our other girl's names; this one's yours."

If Sergei thought anything of the declaration, he said nothing and, instead, lovingly took the chance to name his new daughter. He was quiet for a moment. "Her name is Polina. Polina Sergeyevna Marchenko." Polina means *little one* in Russian. She weighed just five pounds. The name suited her fine. I took a black pen into the nursery during the next visit, and with a shaky fist wrote her name in Cyrillic on the pink card. It was official.

Right away I started to shorten the baby's name to *Polly*. Elaina and Zoya were thrilled with the choice.

"Her name is Polly? Like Polly Pocket, Mom?" Zoya asked.

"Cool!" Elaina was impressed.

Sergei brought Elaina and Zoya up to meet their new sister. He prepped them beforehand at home. They knew that Polly was sick and that she needed to live in a little plastic house in order to get better.

I giggled when they showed up in my hospital room. My mom had put their hair up in high fancy ponytails, but most of it was already falling down. Zoya was wearing Elaina's shirt, two sizes too big. Elaina was squeezed into a pair of Zoya's pajama pants.

"Did you guys get yourselves dressed?" I asked Elaina.

"No, Grandma did," they proclaimed as they strutted into my hospital room. When they came closer for hugs, I noticed they had lipstick on their lips and rubbed into their cheeks like Grandma, too.

"Are you guys ready to meet your sister?" Sergei asked.

"Yeah! We can't wait!"

We walked across the hallway and went into the nursery. I showed them how to put on a blue paper robe over their clothes. Sergei helped them place paper slippers over their shoes. We all counted out loud to sixty while we soaped our hands before rinsing.

Sergei opened the door to Polly's room and Elaina and Zoya saw the incubator. Zoya grabbed my hand.

I bent down so I could see eye to eye with her. "It's okay, Honey," I said. "Polly's in that little house so she can breathe well and stay warm. It's helping her. And she won't be in there forever." *She won't be in there forever,* I coached myself. *She will come home.*

The girls studied Polly. Sergei picked Zoya up so she could see better. "Why doesn't she have any clothes on?" Elaina asked.

"Well, it's warm in the house, so a diaper is all she needs. It's easier for the nurses to give her medicine and other things that way too," Sergei answered.

"Why are her eyes closed?" Zoya wanted to know.

"She's tired," I said. "Her birth was hard for her and now she needs to rest to gain strength."

Both girls seemed fine with our basic answers. They studied her body, counted ten fingers and ten toes and watched the squiggly line on the heart monitor above the incubator.

"Mom, can we go back to your room?" Elaina asked after a few minutes. "We brought coloring books and crayons. I want to color."

"You guys go," Sergei said. "I'll stay and hang out with Polina." Sergei pulled a chair next to Polly and sat down. He opened the incubator window, reached in and placed his pointer finger inside his daughter's small hand. Polly curled her fingers around it.

"Yes, we can go back to the room. We'll come back over and visit Polly a little while later," I said.

We went to my room across the hall and the girls climbed up on the tall bed with me. They opened their backpacks and pulled out Strawberry Shortcake® coloring books and a new pack of Crayola® crayons that Grandma brought for them from America.

"Mom, you're going to color too, right?"

I surveyed my daughters, so healthy, so beautiful. I was glad to see them, and yet I ached in their presence. If Polly had Down syndrome, I would no longer be just an ordinary mom. People would know me as a mother to a child with Down syndrome. What would that mean for my girls? Would Polly embarrass them? Would she become a burden?

"Girls, do you want to go for a walk with me down to the water fountain?" I asked after we had colored for a while.

"Yes, let's go!"

We meandered to the end of the hallway near the nurses' station. Elaina held my left hand and gripped the plastic water pitcher. Zoya walked on the other side of me, fingers laced in mine. I wanted everyone in the hospital to see us. I wanted to show the nurses that I produced healthy, beautiful children. I glanced into other rooms as we walked and saw mothers cooing at their newborns. Many rooms had bouquets of vibrant flowers in glass vases. No one had brought me any flowers. Some moms were watching television, passing time until they could pack up their babies and go home.

I gripped Elaina and Zoya's hands tighter and spoke to them in a loud, attention-grabbing voice. "Isn't it fun at the hospital, girls? Don't you love all the presents Grandma brought from America?" I needed people to see me smile and talk to my kids. *See, I'm a good mom. I make good kids.*

During the first few days in the hospital, friends and family came to visit. Ukrainians brought food. Americans brought cards. My friend Raya brought ice cream and sat on the edge of my bed. She rubbed my feet while I fumbled for words in Russian. When her husband Igor came to pick her up, he stood over Polly's incubator and prayed, "God, if the test for Down syndrome is positive, please heal Polina from it." During his prayer, I shifted my weight. I didn't know much about Down syndrome, but my gut told me it wasn't something like an illness that could be healed.

Over time, visitors continued to tiptoe into Polly's room wearing blue paper robes. Some smiled when they saw her. Others prayed. Many asked questions and got interested in the equipment. I became a tour guide, trying to give answers for our situation. We'd walk back to my room and talk about Polly's scary delivery and her health. I imagined the visitors' sympathy for our misfortune. I imagined prayers on our behalf. Then I imagined them going home, plopping down in front of the television with a nice snack and laughing at a rerun.

The Rock Star doctor entered the nursery and started to speak. It was day six of Polina's life; she had just made me smile by opening her eyes when I cupped her heel. I turned to look at the doctor, "Dobroye Utro," I greeted her in Russian with a smile.

She looked past me. "With disappointment, Gillian, your daughter has Down syndrome."

No *good morning, how are you today.* No, *will your husband be here soon.* Just this, in hurried Russian that I strained to understand: "K sozshaleneyu, Gillian, u vashey dochke seendrom dauna."

I let go of the baby's heel and pulled my hand out of the incubator. The doctor had paused, waiting for my response. "Spaseebo." *Thank you.* I choked out. Then I ran out of the room without looking back at Polina.

In my room across the hall from Polly, nurses surrounded me as I sobbed on my bed. One patted my arm. Another handed me a plastic cup filled with purple liquid. Russian mutterings swirled above me, "Neechevo, perestante kreechat," —*it's nothing, stop crying.* Dazed, I gulped the thick, strong liquid that would soon make me drowsy.

Dr. Rock Star stood closest to my head. "Stop crying!" she ordered. "Yes, it's terrible that your daughter has Down syndrome, but you have options. You can terminate your parenting rights or take her to live in the village. Take her some place quiet. She'll play. Life is slow there. Now, stop crying!"

Everyone around me nodded and patted me, muttering again, "Neechevo, Gillian, neechevo."

It's nothing, Gillian, it's nothing.

9

"Sergei, she has it," I blurted through my tears into the phone.

"What? Who has what?" he asked, confused. He was on his way to the hospital, but I couldn't wait to tell him, so I had called his cell.

"Polly," I cried. "It's Polly. She has it. The doctor told me the test results were positive. She has Down syndrome." I began to sob.

"Oh, Gill. I'm coming. I'll be there as soon as I can. Hold on."

In the bathroom, I splashed my face with water over and over. It took my breath away. Concentrating on the mirror, I noticed I was bright red. A cacophony of thoughts darted in and out of my mind. *Why did you let this happen, God? What do we do now? What kind of mother runs away from her baby? Is that who I am?* Water traveled down my face and dripped onto my nightgown. My sleepy eyes looked dark, almost black, although they are hazel. I studied my facial features—my eyes, my lips, my nose— all small compared to the expanse of my forehead. *This is me. I'm still me.* Water mingled with my tears.

Back on my bed, I sat feeling numb until I heard heavy footsteps coming down the hall. They stopped outside my room and Sergei flung the door open. "Gilly," he murmured, as he threw his green army bag down on the chair. He rushed over to the bed, fell into me, and took me in his arms. He was crying as we drew together, and our sobs caught a rhythm—crescendos and decrescendos, spilling and spilling.

"I don't *want* this, Sergei. I don't *want* this," I said again and again. "I know, Gillian, I know," Sergei rubbed my back with one arm while he embraced me with the other. I tried to place myself anywhere else in my mind where there was still a feeling of life before this, but nothing fit. I wanted to pack an overnight bag and board an airplane and fly all day and night.

"We should go see Polly," Sergei said. I didn't want to see her. Sergei stood up and held his arms out to me and lifted me. When we got inside the sick room, we walked up to the incubator. "There's our girl!" Sergei said with excess enthusiasm.

He opened the incubator door and put his hand on her chest, then bent down as close as he could. His forehead rested against the plastic near hers. "We love you, Polina." He coughed. "Mama and Papa love you."

10

I cut out the words *the sun will shine again* and taped them to the inside cover of my journal.

The words were part of an email in response to our news; it was from a man who had an adult child with Down syndrome. He said he wished people would pray for other things besides Polina not having Down syndrome, because a person either has it or they don't. The email ended by saying, "I grieve for your situation but I do know that the sun will shine again, and you will laugh again. At some point, you would not choose any other child."

The previous morning, I had gone for my first walk outside, at my mom's observation, "You need fresh air." People strolled down the sunny sidewalk. One man had an umbrella tucked under his arm. I'd glanced back at the hospital entrance and seen a woman stepping out the front door. Her husband scrambled as she looked on. He placed their new baby in a car seat at her feet and raced off to get the car. I watched him feel his pockets for keys, jump in the vehicle, then slowly bring it up to his family. All three settled in, and the car drove away. I stood there, arms empty, middle aching. Would we have a day like that any time soon? Would Sergei pull up to the front door and take us home? And if he did, what were we supposed to do then?

Days in the hospital started to run together. I had no outlet. If I had been home, I could have searched online for information about Down syndrome. But in the hospital, it was just us and our fears. The staff had no information to offer, and there were no glossy pamphlets with pictures of happy families holding babies with Down syndrome.

"Let me drive you home," Sergei said one morning. You can see the girls and look up some things on the Internet."

"I don't know if I can leave," I said.

"I checked with the doctor. She's fine with it. And Polly will be fine too. We'll go for two hours. Come on, let's do it." I didn't tell Sergei I wasn't afraid to leave because of Polly. I was afraid to leave because I had to face the fact that one day I would go home with a child who had Down syndrome.

Sergei drove through the streets of Kiev. I peered out the window and watched life happen around us, as if it were a movie. It was a sunny day. I had a headache.

"Mama! Mama!" Elaina and Zoya ran through the apartment towards the front door when they heard the key in the lock. My mom and Sergei's mother, Tatiana, were home with the girls. My mom had been in Ukraine for over two weeks now. As soon as Sergei opened the outside door, I could hear her voice. "Now settle down, Kids, settle down. Remember, your mom's stomach is sore so you have to be gentle."

The inside door opened and the girls' arms were around my waist. "Hi, Girls! It's so nice to see you at home!" I feigned happiness. Elaina and Zoya grinned and giggled. "Kiss me, mom, kiss me," Zoya pleaded. "Zo, I can't bend down. Here, stand on the shoe shelf." Zoya hopped up on the shelf and leaned in to kiss me on the lips. She smelled like chocolate. "Has Grandma been giving you candy?" I asked. The girls exploded into laughter. They were perfect little creatures—the kind of children we expected to have.

Sergei's mom came forward and kissed my cheek. She had been to the hospital a few times to visit, but I hadn't seen her since we learned of Polly's diagnosis. Her face was expressionless. As she moved away, she wiped a tear from her eye. She kissed Sergei next and then slipped out of the fray.

The house didn't look like it was mine. The kids showed me more of the things Grandma brought them from America. My mom, Sergei, Sergei's mom and I all sat in the living room. They talked about Polly's health, how she was eating and sleeping. The girls talked about going for walks outside with Lena.

"Sergei, I'm going to go check the computer. I'll be out in a little while." I went into our bedroom. The room was cold. Surveying the space around me, I exhaled, then sat down at the desk and turned on the computer.

"New Parents to a child with Down syndrome," I typed into the Google search bar. The first link at the top of the page read "Down syndrome: For New Parents, a site dedicated to helping new parents understand Down Syndrome and to appreciate the capabilities of their wonderful child." I blinked back tears and clicked.

At the top of the page was a cherubic angel sitting— her head propped up with her hand, like she was envisioning something dreamy. The quote under the header read: "When you think you have learned what you need to know in life, someone truly special comes in to it and shows you how much more there is."

I started clicking around and went to the Questions and Answers page.

I clicked on the first question: What is Down syndrome?

There was a picture of 23 sets of chromosomes. The caption read: "The chromosomes of a boy with Down syndrome. The arrow points to the extra chromosome 21."

I skimmed the information under the picture and learned that Down syndrome is caused by having three copies of the 21 chromosome, instead of two. All the chromosomes are normal, even the extra one.

Polly had three normal copies of her 21 chromosome. She had more than the rest of us. But what are chromosomes? I learned they are simply the code that contains our hereditary information: Sergei's blue eyes, my fair skin, Polly's blond hair. Chromosomes are given to us by our parents. I started to tap my foot on the wooden floor. *What if I gave her Down syndrome?*

A lot of people coming to the site must have had similar questions about whether they were to blame, because the question was there big as life: "Did I cause my child to have Down syndrome?"

The simple answer, they said, was "No." Down syndrome was fairly shared across all ethnicities and socio-economic levels, in all countries. No relationship between diet or illness and the condition had ever been established.

But I was the one who had wanted another child.

11

Polly gained strength. Her blood infection cleared up and she no longer needed oxygen. One morning, a nurse mentioned that the hospital had a tradition of giving a champagne toast as a way of saying goodbye to the new family.

"But you won't want to have a reception, right? Because your baby has Down syndrome."

Don't cry, Gillian. Don't cry. My whole body tightened. *Speak up. You need to say something.*

"Actually, we would like the reception. Who do I need to talk to in order to set it up?"

The nurse straightened her shirt.

"Oh, you would? Well, okay. I'll let the office know."

A few days later, over thirty people came to the reception to celebrate with us. Once everyone was assembled in the plain white foyer, Sergei and I walked through the steel doors with our daughter. The outfit I brought from home was two sizes too big for Polly, even though it was for a baby 0-6 months old. She slept in my arms while I plastered a smile on my face. I scanned the room, surveying everyone in Kiev who loved us. Did they feel sorry for us? Were they as shocked as I was? But there were flowers and balloons, and everyone fussed over Polly and me.

Standing in the foyer of the Ukrainian hospital with my daughter who had Down syndrome and a room full of people who cared about us, a flicker of hope ignited. Sergei passed around champagne, then offered a prayer for Polly, for us.

"Amen," everyone said. My mom was hugging Zoya. Our whole American team was there with a few missionaries who were in town for meetings. Our dear friends Igor and Raya came. Sergei's mom and dad were there.

After more hugs and well wishes, we piled into our car to go home. We had no car seat, so I held Polly on my lap. She slept in her pink, cotton blanket. Sergei drove while my mom looked out the window and Elaina and Zoya buzzed with excitement. The streets of Kiev were gray and lifeless.

12

Polly was three weeks old the day we brought her home. The next evening, while Sergei was making dinner and my mom was drawing pictures with Elaina and Zoya, the doorbell rang. I was lying on the bed with Polly. She was wearing a cabbage-patch doll outfit I had borrowed from the girls.

"I got it!" Sergei yelled from the kitchen. "Kto tam?" Who's there? I heard a woman's muffled voice and Sergei unlocked the large steel door.

"Hello, I'm the doctor who is assigned to this neighborhood in Kiev. My job is to visit all the new babies after they get home from the hospital. Do you have a few moments for me to examine the child?" By now, I had stood up and come into the foyer. Sergei checked with me and I nodded yes.

"Yes, of course, the baby is right in here." The doctor took her shoes off and followed Sergei into the bedroom. I walked behind her, suddenly nervous.

The doctor set her briefcase down next to our bed and glanced at Polly. "Mozshna pomyt ruki?" *May I wash my hands?*

"Right this way," Sergei said.

I sat down on the bed next to Polly who had just started to wake up. The doctor came back into the room and bent to examine our daughter. Her glasses rested on the edge of her nose as she listened to our baby's heart with her stethoscope. She opened Polly's mouth and peeked in. I watched her hands; she worked carefully and quickly. After she examined Polly, she picked up one of the baby's hands and scrutinized her palm.

After a moment, she placed Polly's hand back on the comforter, stood up and faced Sergei. "You did not know before the baby was born that she had Down syndrome?"

"No, we didn't know beforehand."

"I can't believe the hospital missed it." The doctor gave Polly the once over, then turned her attention to me.

"I'm sorry. They should have caught this mistake before your baby was born so you could have taken care of it."

My lips started to tremble.

Sergei walked to the bed and took my hand. "Oh no, you don't understand. We didn't know that our daughter Polina had Down syndrome before she was born, but if we did know, we still would have had her. We love our child."

The doctor's mouth fell open. She stared at Sergei then back at me. I let go of Sergei's hand and picked up Polly.

"Well, then. I guess that's that. I will call you in a few days to follow up and see how the child is doing."

The doctor turned and walked out of the bedroom.

Once we were discharged from the hospital, my goal was to get back to the States as soon as possible. We made plans to leave within three weeks. Airline tickets were purchased. Sergei rushed around the city tying up loose ends. He passed the baton at church to a new pastor. The lease to our apartment was severed with a handshake. We went to the American embassy to apply for Polly's passport. We put a For Sale sign on the car.

My mom was still with us. "I'm here as long as you need me." Every day she gave me measurable projects in fifteen-minute increments. "Clean out this drawer. Pack the kids' underwear." The boxes that held the belongings we were leaving behind were going to be stored at my friend Alyona's, just outside the city.

I packed knickknacks, toys and clothes, and marveled at the amount of stuff we had accumulated living in Kiev for three and a half years. When we arrived in 2003, we came with two small children and six suitcases. Since then I had found enough treasures to fill our two-bedroom apartment.

I made piles: give, store, take. I gave dishes and pots to my Ukrainian friends. I found a ministry that helped new moms without an income and donated two boxes of Elaina and Zoya's clothes. I packed the girls' keepsake books and prized toys. "We'll come back one day and get your stuffed animals and dolls," I told Elaina. "I know, let's leave this special box at Babushka's house. She'll watch your dolls for you." Elaina cried when we taped up the box.

Our take pile was the smallest. We were leaving Ukraine much like we had come; with our children, legal documents, and a few clothes and other personal belongings.

The life we built in Ukraine was being broken down as easily as a cardboard box. Our church in Michigan wrote and said they had temporary housing available. Would we like to stay there when we returned? It was a huge relief knowing we had some place to go while we tried to reclaim a life in the States. And the house was just fifteen minutes from my parent's house.

"Gill, did you get the dresser cleaned out in the girls' bedroom?" My mom was standing behind me. I didn't hear her come up. Elaina and Zoya were playing with their Barbies on the lower bunk bed. Sergei was at work. Polly was in the living room, sleeping in her bassinet. I was a mom of three. I was a wife. I was thirty-one years old.

All I wanted was to go home.

13

Boxes were stacked floor-to-ceiling along the walls. The room was no longer familiar. Knickknacks and paintings were packed away. I was alone with the baby when Tanya came to visit.

Tanya and I were acquaintances, having met a few months back when she came to church with a friend. Entertaining a guest right now did not top my to-do list but she had phoned consistently since Polly was born. *When was a good time to come by?* I put her off several times and finally gave in. Tanya didn't speak English. I was tired and my Russian was sloppy.

A young professional in her early 20s, Tanya worked as a dentist. She wasn't married. She opened the bottle of wine she'd brought over and poured me half a glass. Handing me the drink, she asked shyly, "Mozshna vzyat rebyonka?" *May I hold the baby?* I handed Polly to Tanya and showed her how to support the baby's head with her elbow. We settled down in the living room, and I took a sip of the dark, red wine. It warmed my throat as it went down.

"I don't know much about Down syndrome, so I went online and did some research before I came. I read an article that talked about the importance of early therapy for the child. And they say there are now special vitamins that can help a baby with Down syndrome get stronger."

I was surprised. Tanya was talking about topics I didn't expect people in Ukraine to know about. She asked thoughtful questions and tilted her head towards me while she cuddled Polly.

"You know, Gillian, I've never met someone with Down syndrome. I don't think I've ever seen a person with Down syndrome in Kiev. It's rare to see a person with any sort of disability here."

"That's what I've heard. Someone told me about a couple who brought their son with Down syndrome to church. A man came up to them after the service and told them that an extra chromosome meant their child was smarter than other kids. He said the boy would be a genius." Tanya and I started to chuckle as I took another sip of wine.

So far, none of my Ukrainian friends talked to me about Polly having Down syndrome because they simply did not know what to say. My American friends did talk about it, putting their positive spin on the situation. All the Americans had stories about kids with Down syndrome. I heard about kids who went to college, others who lived on their own, held jobs and made their own lunches. The first time I talked to my brother Justin in California, he reminded me of the show I loved in middle school that starred a guy with Down syndrome named Corky. Another friend told me about a girl he knew who was a real cool kid. "She can talk and everything," he'd said.

Our conversation lulled, and Tanya and I sat in comfortable silence, drinking our wine.

The next day, we went to our last church service. Every week for the past few months, we'd paraded in with our props, a whole church in a box, to set up a service in a rented building that used to house a school for the blind.

That morning, I walked in with Polly. She was six pounds, dressed from head to toe in white—complete with a white bonnet falling over her forehead, hiding her button nose and making it difficult to see the wide space between her eyes.

We took communion at our church every week. Today, I held Polly. My legs wobbled when I stood after everyone else went forward. I stepped towards the front, preparing to receive communion from my husband and my pastor, one and the same.

"The bread of Christ," Sergei said in Russian, holding out a cubed piece of white bread. I began to cry. Polly was like a brick in my arms. I could not say "Amen."

"The bread of Christ," Sergei whispered. His eyes pierced mine, urging me to take the bread.

I remembered my first communion years ago as a child, when I'd been so excited to take the bread for the very first time. How could I have known my life would turn out like this? I cried harder. I imagined everyone in the service leaning forward, urging me to take the bread. *Accept this, Gillian. Accept this.*

I gritted my teeth. Holding Polly and trembling, I willed myself to do what seemed unimaginable. Sergei was waiting.

"Amen," I whispered.

And I swallowed the cube of stale, white bread.

14

We touched down on American soil: five suitcases, three children, two exhausted parents, and a single infinite sadness. All through the trip, I had tried to avoid the eyes of strangers, had felt that everyone who looked at Polly must know. If I could just get home, maybe the sting of Down syndrome would ease.

"Next!" the passport control officer bellowed. We gathered up our bags and children and moved forward to the desk. My hand shook as I placed our five passports on the counter. The officer picked up each one checking our information and matching faces to pictures. His eyes rested no longer on Polina than anyone else.

"Okay, you are all good, folks." He met my gaze, "Welcome home."

We had arranged for my sister Amy to pick us up at the airport. She is five years older than I am, and we don't resemble each other at all. She has black hair and I am a blonde. Her skin is olive. Mine is pasty white. When I was little, a five-year difference felt more like twenty. I wanted Amy's attention. She knew how to play me, too. "Gill, I'll trade you this empty tissue box for the necklace Grandma gave you for Christmas." "Okay!" I'd sing out, thrilled to get anything from my big sister.

Amy loved to have her head scratched. Sometimes at night I'd strike her a deal. "I'll scratch your head if you talk to me." We'd lie there together and I would scratch and she'd say whatever came to mind. If she'd stop talking, I'd stop scratching.

My parents would be downstairs watching the nine o'clock news. But, up in the stillness, I didn't worry lying next to my sister.

Amy got married when she was nineteen years old. Her first child came along a year later. I remember watching her with the baby, in awe of him and how beautiful he was. Sometimes I got to lie with him on the couch. He'd sprawl across my chest and sleep, warming me from within. I started to daydream about having a child of my own someday.

When our plane landed at O'Hare, there was no way to call Amy and tell her we were there, since we had no cell phone. In an email, we had said we'd meet her at the drop off and pick up. As soon as we got outside, her black SUV pulled up and Amy got out. I was holding Polly, but I reached with one arm to hug my sister. "This is Polly," I whispered. I somehow needed Amy in this moment, the way I'd needed her when I was five. I watched her eyes.

"Hi, Polly," Amy said with hesitation, then looked away. She didn't hug or kiss or offer to take the baby.

Amy's excitement went up ten notches as she corralled her nieces for hugs. Was this how the rest of the family would act too? I shook off how I felt. *I am just being sensitive*, I thought. *I'm tired.*

"Girls, would you like a snack?" Amy was prepared for our two-hour trip to Michigan from Chicago. She had packed a small cooler of snacks and drinks. Elaina and Zoya snapped open individual bags of potato chips and Canada Dry. They were excited about America, having remembered our last trip home two years before. It had been all fun and family, and they were spoiled. Now, they made jokes with Aunt Amy and jabbered on about seeing Grandma and Grandpa, forgetting they traveled halfway around the world and hadn't slept for twenty-four hours. Polly and Sergei both slept in the car, and I counted the minutes. I couldn't wait to get home.

We pulled into the driveway at my folks' house and I felt myself exhale. Two days ago, at the beginning of our journey in Ukraine, I'd decided it was up to me to get us home. It was as if I'd taken the steering wheel from Sergei and from the pilots on the planes. It took all that was in me, a kind of hanging-by-my-claws type of exertion, to will our little family up into the air, over an ocean and finally into the driveway of my parents' home.

My mom and dad were at the car window before I could unbuckle a kid from a booster. Amy's kids were there, too: Will, Karli, and Ben. Lil' Gram, my mother's mom, who had been living with my parents for the last ten years, was standing at the door with her walker, waiting for us to come inside. I got Polly out of her car seat and turned around into my dad's arms. He hugged us close.

After everyone greeted and embraced us, we piled into my parents' house. Lil' Gram held me and cried. She leaned down and kissed Polly on the forehead, while Elaina and Zoya fought over who would get to push her walker around first.

I waited for the load I'd carried home to lift off my shoulders, but Polly started to fuss and cry. The girls ran circles through the house—the kitchen, the hallway, the dining room, the living room. Sergei settled onto the couch and closed his eyes. Amy and her kids lounged in chairs and on the floor. I took the baby into a back bedroom and laid her on the bed.

"Is she okay?" my dad asked, walking up behind us.

"She's fine. She needs her diaper changed."

Standing there with my father behind me and my new baby lying on the bed, I wanted him to say something. Maybe, "I'm glad you are home, Gill" or "Boy, you've been through a lot."

I studied my daughter and wondered if she weighed closer to seven pounds now. My dad had caught fish bigger than that. She looked frail. Her face was not the usual baby pink. In some spots her skin was translucent. If she were a freshly-painted room, she would have needed a second coat. *Did my family regard her as sickly? Did they see a child with Down syndrome? Were they frightened of her?* I wanted to ask my dad while he stood next to me. I didn't dare, though, because I was afraid of his answers to my questions. Or more afraid that he wouldn't answer, that he'd blow me off with something pat like, "She's fine." I kept quiet.

Back in the living room with everyone, I thought I sensed my family's apprehension around the baby. I watched Elaina sitting up on her grandpa's lap. He was playing creepy crawler with her, a game he used to play with me. He walked his fingers up her leg like a spider, then sprang up to tickle her neck. Elaina giggled. "Again!" she cried. "Again!"

Something in me shifted.

We had plans to stay at my mom and dad's house for dinner, but I wanted to leave. Polly was crying and my eyes were crossing from jet lag. A temporary home in a neighboring town had been prepared for us. I wanted to go there. I wanted to feed Polly and put the girls to bed. I wanted to sleep for a year.

"Mom, we're going to go."

"You sure? Dinner is almost ready. I made a roast."

I peeked into the dining room. A gold tablecloth covered the table. The dishes were set for a meal.

"Yeah, I'm sure. Polly is tired. We all need to sleep." My mom and I had talked about this homecoming dinner. I had wanted it, even though I wasn't sure we'd be up to it.

My mom offered to box up the food, but I refused.

"No, we'll be fine. Thanks, though."

She gave me a hug and a look of quiet understanding.

I had thought I would feel better here. Growing up, my parents made us sit down every day at five o'clock for dinner; eating together was something I could count on. While in the hospital in Kiev with Polly, I had dreamt of this possibility; my mom's home-cooked meal would take me back to a time when things were simple.

But I could not be fixed by a meal at my childhood home.

The temporary house was in St. Joe, a town fifteen minutes away. It was right next to the church that owned it. When we pulled into the driveway, our friend Carla was waiting with the keys. I noticed she was pregnant. This was her third child, too. Our oldest daughters, Elaina and Erin were one day apart in age. "You're expecting! I didn't know!" I tried to sound upbeat.

"Yes, I didn't get a chance to tell you in the midst of all our emails back and forth." Carla gave me a long hug and put the keys in my hands. "We'll catch up later. For now, you guys get some rest." With a wave of her hand, she got into her car and left.

We went into the house. On the kitchen table sat a bouquet of roses with a lit candle next to it. I walked into the living room and sat Polly down in her car seat. Sergei walked through the rest of the house—two bedrooms and a small bathroom—

and turned on lights. "Wow, it's all set up. The beds are made," he said.

"Mom, Mom, look, it's our room!" cried the girls. Their room was small but managed to hold bunk beds in one corner and a crib for Polly along the other wall. "Mom! Look! Presents!" Elaina crawled up to the top bunk. Zoya dove onto her bed. There were large gift bags with colorful tissue paper sprouting out the tops. "Mom, look, a frog! A monkey!" The girls each pulled out fluffy stuffed animals and hugged them. I saw a dresser with six drawers in the opposite corner of the room. I opened the top drawer. Someone had placed pairs of pajamas for each girl, all the right sizes. I checked the other drawers. They were filled with clothes.

"Hey, the kitchen cupboards and the refrigerator are stocked with food," Sergei called out from the other room. "We're set for a while." I sat on the thin carpet in the girls' room and put my head in my hands.

"Mom, why are you crying?" Elaina asked. Both girls climbed off their beds and crawled into my lap.

"What?" I smiled at my kids through tears. "Oh, I'm glad we're here, that's all."

This was what I was looking for. A space to lick our wounds.

About an hour later, a friend showed up and left us a roast beef dinner. We sat at the table and ate together—a family.

I started to have a glass of white wine every night on the porch. The porch was enclosed and faced the neighbor's yard—about an acre of shaded, green grass and tall pine trees. It reminded me of my grandparent's place, my father's folks, up in northern Michigan in a town called Oscoda. On the porch, no one could tag me out. I spent hours either hiding from my daughters or seeking information about Down syndrome. I felt safe there.

Elaina and Zoya didn't seem to notice my retreat. They were well fed and loved by Sergei and my family. There were a plethora of cartoons in English. They got to go to Grandma's house every few days and my sister stopped by the house often.

The girls were allowed to play outside in the huge backyard by themselves, a major difference from Kiev, where they weren't allowed to step foot outside without an adult. They'd come in after being outdoors, bend down and kiss Polly on her forehead as she sat in a bouncy chair, and then run off again to play.

I watched Elaina and Zoya love Polly and wished I could emulate them. Instead, I woke up emotionally exhausted every day. I'd drive to Target to buy something, make circles inside the store, and come home without the thing I needed. I couldn't think clearly.

It was the beginning of June when we settled into our loaner house. Polly was almost two months old. Sergei, tired of idleness, busied himself around the house. Every morning he got up, changed and fed the baby, poured the girls their cereal and put on a pot of coffee. By the time I'd get out of bed, the kids were settled in watching a cartoon or playing outside. Polly would be lying on a blanket on the floor surrounded by toys she was too little to acknowledge, and Sergei would be sitting in a chair in the living room, his bible laid out on his lap.

He was concerned about work. "Do you think we'll go back to Ukraine? Should we let that part of our lives go? I don't know if I can be successful as a minister in America."

I would sigh and nod. His thoughts were too far ahead. I wasn't considering the future. I couldn't. It was a scary place, focused on the fact that I would mother an ever-aging disabled child. I couldn't think about the household of boxes we packed away and stored in Ukraine. I was busy worrying about the immediate future, like how I was going to get through tomorrow.

We started to orbit in different universes, my husband and I. It was a major change from our time in the hospital in Ukraine, when we clung to each other upon hearing that our daughter had Down syndrome. Sergei involved himself in prayer and action and pondering what we might learn from Polly, and I wallowed in depression on the porch.

After one of his action trips, Sergei had come home from the store with a six-pack of beer and six bottles of wine.

"Whoa, that's a lot of wine!" I'd said, while I unpacked the groceries.

"Yeah, I know. But there was a good sale if you bought six bottles, so I figured I'd get it and we'd have it for dinner parties and company. It will probably last us forever."

After a while, it was much more relaxing if I poured myself a second glass. So I did. I spent countless hours online now, reading stories on the Down syndrome support forum. I'd take a drink of wine and look for pretty moms, moms with blond highlights in chic clothes. They hugged their children with disabilities. They looked happy, like I used to be in pictures with Elaina and Zoya. Soon it was three glasses a night and more internet cruising. *See, I can do this. She's doing it.*

But I wanted to hide from Sergei and the kids. I wanted to hide from my parents who were overly optimistic about Polly and cautious in my presence. I wanted to hide from my friends in town who either acted like nothing happened or wanted every detail.

Once in a while my cell phone would ring but I hardly ever answered it. When I did, it was usually a friend and if I was drinking I'd sound confident on the phone, which elicited praise, "Wow, you sound so good, so together. You guys are handling this situation well."

At night, I'd fall into bed, thankful for a reprieve, eight hours of escape. But even asleep my mind didn't stop churning, making vivid dreams. One had me calling a friend all night long, each time messing up the phone number by one digit. In another dream, I was trying to get to a high school math class, but I couldn't find the room, or I was in the right room but I didn't have a pencil for a test, or I was at my high school graduation and realized I hadn't attended math classes for four years. I would dream about being in the hospital giving birth to Polly. I could feel the cold surgery gurney as I watched the doctors busy at work. At some point every night, Sergei would nudge me awake. "Gilly, you're grinding your teeth again."

I began sneaking wine and drinking in the basement, so Sergei wouldn't notice how much I was having. While he was busy upstairs with the kids, or watching something on television or reading, I would refill glass after glass. Now it was more than just a relaxed cloudy feeling. I could block out all thoughts, and spin around and around in my head and secretly grin at my ability to escape.

One night after four or five glasses of wine, I went in search of Polly. I wanted to hold her. I stumbled up from the basement. My head was swirling and I swallowed repeatedly to keep the wine from crawling up my throat. The soft light above the kitchen sink lit a path into the living room where I got distracted by the glow of the television set with its hum of muffled words. Then I remembered where I was going. I slipped past my sleeping husband sprawled out on the scratchy couch into the bedroom where my three daughters slept.

"Where are you, Polly?" I slurred aloud in the darkness. The room smelled like little girl sweat, sweet and pungent. The top bunk bed squeaked as Elaina rearranged her sleeping self. I reached my hand out sideways to the wall for balance. Cool and smooth to the touch, I felt around for the light switch but couldn't find it. I knew Polly's crib stood directly in front of me. I took a long step, reached out and braced myself against the white railing. My eyes had adjusted to the dark and I could see my baby fast asleep, her stomach rising and falling with each breath. As I reached down to pick her up, she stirred a bit flopping to the side and slipping in my grip. I caught her up and she settled fast on my shoulder. "There's my girl," I said patting her back. Her hair smelled of baby shampoo but her pajamas had a faint musty odor. I'd forgotten to switch the laundry again.

Though I was shaky on my feet, I held her for a while like that with the blanket of night and a cheap bottle of Chardonnay covering up my fears and grief. In moments like those, I was sure I could parent Polly well.

"See, I can do it," I announced to my sleeping children.

In pictures of Polly and me at that time, I look disoriented, like I smoked pot or hadn't slept for five days. Polly is bird-like. I have a forced, tired smile with empty eyes and I'm wearing pajama pants and an old t-shirt. My hair is dull and greasy.

It wasn't long before I was drinking a bottle of wine a night. It helped me sleep. Six bottles were gone in no time.

I noticed Sergei walking out the door with the car keys in his hand one morning, "If you're going to the store, could you pick up some wine?"

"We're out already? What happened to the six bottles we had?"

"I don't know. I guess we drank it. And remember we had company over for dinner twice?"

Sergei didn't pay attention. "Oh, okay. You want white?"

"Yes, white."

I started waking up every night at around four o'clock, parched and sweating, but cold. I'd have a headache. Sometimes my head was still spinning. I'd get up and drink two glasses of water and then lie back down. *Gillian, what are you doing? Why did you drink so much?* I'd think about the people at the church next door who cared so well for our family. They provided the house, free of rent and paid our utilities. We still received a paycheck through the mission group that sent us to Ukraine. People all over the United States were supporting us. *Last time, God, I promise.*

By seven o'clock the next night, I would open another bottle.

I was afraid someone would stop by during the day and see the evidence left out on the counter. No matter how tipsy I got, I made sure I put the wine bottles far down into the trashcan. If the trashcan was empty, I'd place the bottle in the bottom, then pull paper towels off the roll, bunch them up and throw them on top.

"Haven't you had enough?" Sergei would ask once in a while, irritated.

"What? I've had a couple glasses. I'm fine," I'd lie, while trying not to stumble on my way back to the kitchen for another refill.

"Hey, what are you doing right now," I'd play, as he sat in the living room watching *Law and Order* reruns. Seducing him was a way to get past him now.

"Nothing, what are you doing?" he'd ask, interested.

"I think… I am going to bed," I'd smile. "Would you like to come?"

"Absolutely," he'd grin. He forgot about my drinking.

Sergei was in his world and I was in mine. His new baby had Down syndrome too. He forfeited his career and country to bring his family to a place that would provide support for us. I was a mother hiding from my disabled daughter in a bottle of wine.

One Sunday, I sat in the 11 a. m. church service, hung over. While fighting the urge to puke, I bowed my head during prayer like everyone else. But I could not pray, because my head was still spinning. *Oh my gosh! Am I drunk in church?*

Two days later, I thought about having a mid-morning drink, just a sip or two to help me settle down, as the kids colored pictures of butterflies and ladybugs at the kitchen table and Polly took her morning nap. I refrained but it bothered me that I'd wanted it.

On Thursday, my friend Liz from Ukraine, the one who split the *hata* with us, called to check in. "How are you?"

I was sitting in our makeshift bedroom, a small box of a room with a sliding mirror closet door. The window was open. I could hear Zoya hysterical over a knock-knock joke Elaina just told outside on the swing set my dad bought for them.

"I'm, um, not so good. I'm not reading the bible at all and I don't feel like praying. I'm drinking more than I have in my entire life."

"A few glasses of wine aren't the end of the world. You're going through a huge transition. Grieving is natural." A wave of thankfulness washed over me. She loved me.

"But listen, you can't stop reading scripture. You can't stop praying. You are going through a difficult time. But you don't get to take a pass when it comes to your faith. This is the time you need God most."

I sat up straighter on my bed. The word *pass* ticked in my head like a pesky metronome.

That's what I was doing; I was trying to take a pass on my new life.

I wanted to tell Liz I was afraid of my child and, in fact, I was now afraid of my life. I could not stop drinking because I would have to try to love Polly on my own, without a manufactured glow of happiness to pull me towards her. Without alcohol, I couldn't take her in my arms and claim that gooey, newborn love—the wonder of new baby toes and the joy of shampooed baby hair. The stuff that a new mom should feel. The stuff I was void of.

I couldn't speak. Too many thoughts rushed into my mind. Liz was right. You can't clock in and out of motherhood like it's a job, and head to some obscure resort in the Mexico of your mind.

"Gillian, are you still there?"

"Yeah, I'm here," I whispered.

"You know we love you guys, don't you?"

"Of course."

"I'll call you next week to see how you are doing."

"Okay, thanks." I hung up and fell back on the bed. Sergei was outside playing with the kids. Polly was asleep in her crib in the other room. I rolled over and cried myself to sleep.

Once during my college days in Chicago, I saw a ruined car on the side of the road. It was smashed up. The driver's door almost touched the passenger's door on the other side because it was so bent in. It was rusted out and broken. Hanging inside, from the rear view mirror, was an air freshener shaped like a pine tree. The car was totaled, but at least it still smelled pine fresh.

My life as Polina's mother was the reverse of that car. I was smashed up inside, but on the outside I did my best to seem fresh. I was such a fantastic fake that no one knew the extent of my grief. No one knew how I struggled to love Polly or that I was drinking to escape.

The morning after I talked to Liz, I picked up my bible and held it in my hands.

All you have to do is read.

I opened it to the book of Psalms, remembering the psalm I read in the hospital the day we took Polly home.

I felt okay about reading a psalm, because every other one exposes a depressed author. I opened to Psalm 84, then underlined a portion: "Even the sparrow finds a home there, and the swallow builds her nest and raises her young at a place near your altar." Even a bird, a thing that eats worms, knew to draw near to its maker. While I read this verse, I realized I had been isolating myself from God.

I decided to try to read a psalm a day. I wanted to pray as well, but "God, please help" was all I could muster. I brought the laptop to the living room and stopped hiding out in the basement. I still drank at night, but less.

Over time, something started to surface in my conscious-ness: alcohol-drenched emotions were false. While drinking, I didn't love Polly any better. I didn't love her at all.

I hid the corkscrew in the back of a kitchen drawer.

I made an appointment with Dr. Peterson, the pediatrician who had cared for Elaina and Zoya. In Kiev I had wished for this. I wanted American doctors to examine Polly and explain Down syndrome to me in English. I wanted to understand why the presence of an extra chromosome in her body fouled up all the directions, making some things difficult for her to do, and other things impossible.

Polly sat in her car seat at my feet in the waiting room as I filled out her new patient paperwork. I answered each question, printing in a steady hand. *Name, Address, City and State.* Polly gurgled. I rocked her car seat back and forth with my foot, while two kids next to us played with a mish mash of waiting-room toys.

Other moms sat scattered around the room while their children played with toys and read books. When we'd first walked in I had searched the faces of the kids, scanning to see if anyone had visible special needs.

Sibling: Names and ages. Easy. I jotted the answers. With the first page complete, I dated it, signed my name and flipped to the other side. *History. Does your child have, or has she/he ever had…* Most of the descriptions under this heading were either inconsequential or did not apply. *Ear infections, allergies, menstrual period, diabetes, acne?* But there were a few that started to make me sweat. *Problem hearing?* Maybe. *Problem seeing?* I didn't know, but her eyes jiggled and she was bad at making eye contact. *Blood transfusion?* Yes, but I had no idea why. No one in Ukraine ever told me more than "she had an infection." *What mother doesn't know these things?* I zoomed through the rest of the list expecting something like *mental retardation*, but it wasn't there. I didn't know what to do, so I wrote *Down syndrome* under *Other Concerns.* By the time I finished the new patient form, sweat was dripping down my nose and my hands were shaking.

"Polina?" a nurse in pale pink scrubs with kittens on them stood at the door. I picked up the car seat and went forward. "Hello, how are you?" she said.

"Fine, thanks," I said. *I don't want to tell you how I really am.*

We were taken to an exam room where I undressed Polly. She was weighed and measured. The nurse told me her stats as she wrote them down but I didn't pay attention. After she left I held Polly, wrapped in a plaid blue fleece blanket, and waited for Dr. Peterson.

I liked this doctor. He was a grandfather type and resembled Abe Lincoln. Honest Abe. He had been gentle and kind with Elaina and Zoya. In the past, he had taken his time with me, answering all the questions I'd had regarding my kids. He and his wife belonged to one of the churches in the area that gave us money to go to Ukraine as missionaries. I was anxious to talk to Dr. Peterson because he was a kind doctor and a person of faith. Surely, he'd see the value in Polly and encourage me in my new role.

"Gillian! So nice to see you again!" Dr. Peterson opened the door to our room. I stood up awkwardly and gave him a quick hug. He was surprised by my hug. I scolded myself internally.

"This must be Polina. Can I hold her?"

"Sure," I handed Polly over.

"Hello Polina. We've been praying for you." Dr. Peterson's church had gotten the email updates Sergei sent out about Polly in Ukraine. "Now, let me take a look."

He laid her in his lap and carefully unfolded the fleece blanket, then started to move her legs like she was riding a bicycle. He checked her ears and shined a light in her eyes. "How's her heart?" he asked as he took the stethoscope around his neck into his hand to warm it up before placing it over her heart.

"Good. I don't have the details, but it was checked in Ukraine and the doctor said she didn't have any defects."

"That's great. It will help a lot. Most of these kids usually have some kind of hole in their hearts. Often times it will close up on its own, but sometimes surgery is required."

These kids. Dr. Peterson's wording bothered me, but I understood what he was saying.

He finished his exam, wrapped Polly back up and handed her to me.

"There is a separate growth chart for these kids. I'll have a nurse find one. I don't have it with me today."

Again, *these kids.* I smiled and nodded. I knew that already. I had brought one with me but decided to keep it to myself.

"Typically, these kids tend to have extra medical concerns. You'll need to have her hearing and eyesight checked, for sure. There are other things to check. I'll do some research and let you know."

I already know. I have the growth chart for kids with Down syndrome in my purse. I have an updated medical check list as well. It took me two minutes to find online. The carpet in the exam room seemed to come alive, like it was opening up to swallow Polly and me whole.

"Um, Polly has surprised us so far. She is starting to look us in the eye. She's eating well and she sleeps well. She's a lot like Elaina and Zoya were."

"Good, good. That's great. You know, these kids usually

develop normally to a certain level, maybe to a kindergartener or a first grader, and then they stop developmentally. In my experience, once they stop you can't help them develop more. These kids will usually do better in special needs schools."

Dr. Peterson concentrated on my face. Was this sympathy? Did he assume he was consoling me? I was a mother to a child who had Down syndrome, trying hard not to categorize my baby as one of *these kids*. Dr. Peterson mistook my tears. "Hang in there. We're praying for you. I want to see Polly back in a month, to keep an eye on her growth. Okay?"

"Okay … um, thank you."

"You bet." Dr. Peterson stood up. "Is there anything else you want to discuss?"

"No, I think we're done. Thanks."

He closed the door and I got Polly dressed and put her in her car seat. I should have said something. But what? I had been sure people would treat Polly differently in the United States, but now here I was standing in the middle of an American examination room, feeling exactly the way I'd felt in Ukraine. I knew Dr. Peterson. He was a good doctor and he cared about people. Still, a few weeks later, we switched to a different pediatrician.

I had read about the growth chart and common medical issues in the book, *Babies with Down syndrome: A New Parent's Guide.* It came free in a packet mailed to us by a local Down syndrome support group, after I found their website and requested information. Below the title of the book it said, "The first book that parents and family should read."

I used to love the NBC commercials about the importance of knowledge. Someone famous would say something wise about reading, or exercising or eating right and the music would cue. *The more you know...* and the star would shoot across the screen. Knowledge *would* give me power but it seemed far away and getting there felt like walking across shards of glass, cutting my feet with each step.

I opened the book. On the first page, it read, "The best way to understand Down syndrome—what it means to your baby and what it means to you—is to get the facts. For a condition that has for so long been shrouded in fear and darkness, the facts are far better than the myths. The worst enemy facing parents of babies with Down syndrome is ignorance. Before you do anything or decide anything about your baby, learn about Down syndrome."

I scanned the first few pages to review what I had learned about Down syndrome in Kiev. "What is Down syndrome: Down syndrome means that your baby has one extra chromosome in each of his millions of cells. Instead of 46, he has 47. Over six thousand babies with Down syndrome are born in the United States every year and thousands more in other countries. It occurs in boys and girls evenly. It is one of the most common birth defects, occurring in all races, ethnic groups, socio-economic classes, and nationalities. It can happen to anyone."

It can happen to anyone.

I understood it could happen to anyone, but it didn't just happen to anyone, it happened to me. Women get pregnant and have perfect children. There had been a time in my life when hard things happened only to other people. That time was over.

I read the first five chapters in one sitting. I read with horror and hope. I sobbed every time I read the word "retardation" and gasped when I learned that kids with Down syndrome were more prone to childhood cancer. *I don't want Polly to have anything else. Isn't Down syndrome enough?*

One morning when Zoya was only a year and a half old, Elaina, then three, came into our bedroom, crawled up between Sergei and me, and placed her hand on my chest.

"Mom, Zoya's crying."

"I hear her, Lainie."

"Well, then, get up and get her."

"Elaina, I will. I just don't want to get up this second."

She was silent for a moment. "Mom, you shouldn't have had kids if it's too hard for you."

Maybe Elaina had been right. I shouldn't have had children. This was just too hard for me.

A week after our visit to Dr. Peterson, I made a phone call to Early Intervention, a federal support system of services for children ages 0-3 with disabilities. I talked to a polite woman named Jennifer who set up a meeting at our home with a social worker.

The day Lila the social worker came, I dressed Polly up in a cute pink and brown outfit and laid her down on a fresh blanket in the middle of the living room. Sergei took Elaina and Zoya to the park so it would be quiet. I changed my shirt a few times and fussed over my hair, nervous about talking to the social worker. Would I babble on and on like she was a bartender? Would I sit and stare at my hands? Would I break down crying? Would she judge me? Would I know what questions to ask?

Lila was tall with a wispy, thin build. She had blond hair

that hung to her shoulders. She sat on the sunken green couch and explained the early intervention program. "A team of therapists will come to your home for an initial evaluation of Polly. There will be four or five people: a physical therapist, a speech therapist, an occupational therapist, your assigned case worker and possibly a developmental therapist."

Polly cooed on her blanket. Her hand searched for a red and orange rattle. She found it and brought it to her mouth.

"The team will do an evaluation and assess Polly's therapeutic needs. Since she has Down syndrome, she automatically qualifies for therapy, but we'll assess globally what therapies are required and how often and for how long."

Polly was nine weeks old. What kind of therapy could they do with a baby who was just starting to see faces?

I tried to stop my hand from shaking every time Lila gave me a paper to sign. After a half hour of going over Polina's medical history, including my pregnancy, her birth and her health to date, Lila left as easily as she had come.

"Thanks for coming." I closed the door and watched her walk through the enclosed porch. The screen door smacked shut. It was Polly and me now, the house still and quiet. I went back to the living room and picked her up from the floor. "Well, we did it, huh? What's next, I wonder? Do you know?" Polly keyed in on my face, her eyes searching, always searching like she was watching for a light to switch on in my eyes. I sat down on the couch and held her close and cried.

The next Thursday a developmental team came to evaluate Polly. The group of therapists showed up at one o'clock sharp.

They came through the door with stuffed briefcases and cloth tote bags bursting with rattles and board books. The five women reminded me of an entourage of Secret Service agents protecting the president. It seemed too much for a ten-week-old baby.

Once situated in the living room, each therapist took a turn evaluating Polly through play. They sought to see if she made eye contact (she could); if she tracked toys with her eyes (she did for a few seconds); if she was able to bring her hands together midline (which she did in order to hold her favorite rattle). But because Polly was still so tiny, the therapists mostly talked to us. They wrote goals for her for the next six months—things like, "Polly will look in the direction of a voice calling her name."

I was lost. Finding a person's face when your name was called was never taught to Elaina and Zoya. We didn't need goals with them. Things just happened. It was typical growth. Kids live and grow. Walking and talking and learning to tie shoes are relatively easy abilities to achieve. But there's the difference: typical growth—and Polly wasn't typical.

"Do you agree with these goals?" our new caseworker asked. We nodded and signed dotted lines showing our approval.

It was decided that Polly would have four therapy sessions a week in our home. Our job was to reinforce for the rest of the week the exercises the therapists showed us during each session. After two hours of testing and decision-making, the therapy team paraded out of the house. Polly was fast asleep on her blanket on the floor.

"Well, Polly's going to be the busiest baby on the block, that's for sure," said Sergei as he plopped down on the couch.

How were we going to manage everything?

I reluctantly made an appointment with a pediatric eye doctor. I knew Polly had eye troubles. They'd jiggle back and forth, and sometimes they would cross when she looked you in the face. At the doctor's we found out Polly was far-sighted. She also had an astigmatism, a weak eye, and nystagmus.

It didn't faze me when the doctor said Polly needed glasses. I made a sassy joke about her being cute enough to pull off a pair of glasses. The doctor and nurse both chuckled. They seemed pleased that I was so together. Their laughter was affirming. Every time I could convince people around me that I was okay with having a child with Down syndrome, it convinced me for a few moments, too.

As Polly and I were getting ready to leave, I noticed an older man sitting in the waiting room, watching us. Before we were called in, he'd been tuned in to us as well, but I'd thought nothing of it. Now I scrutinized him. He was dressed in a flannel shirt and wore a dusty baseball cap. Tufts of salt and pepper hair stuck out around the rim of his hat. He looked like a man who could have worked construction his whole life. Why was he staring at us?

I bent down to stuff Polly's arms into her snowsuit and sensed someone walking up behind me. The man cleared his throat and I jumped a little. I stood up and turned around. His jaw was set and his gaze was firm.

"Take good care of her," he said.

"Excuse me?"

He didn't blink. "I said, take good care of her."

What was he talking about? After a few beats, he said, "I had a brother-in-law whose parents treated him horribly."

He glanced down at Polly. Tears sprung to my eyes.

"Of course I'll take care of her."

He looked at Polly again and back to me, then sat down and nodded to me before picking up a magazine to read.

My eyes burned and a flash of heat wormed up my neck. I crouched down to Polly.

"Polly, you know I love you, right?" My declaration of love sounded more like a bad break up line, but I nuzzled her and kissed the wide, flat space between her eyes.

I was shaking as I turned to leave. Of course I was going to take care of my child! Even when I was deep in grief the issue was never *if* I would care for Polly. I'd thought about what caring for her might do to me, but I had never considered treating her poorly. I rushed out to the car, clicked Polly into her car seat base, and planted another obligatory kiss on her head.

The cold air almost knocked me over as I emerged from the back seat and stood up. I had raced out of the office forgetting to zip up my winter coat. Scrambling to get into the driver's seat, I put the key into the ignition, locked the doors, blasted the heat, and burst into sobs.

Who was I kidding? I was a terrible mother for Polly. A stranger could see that. So what if I always cared for her basic needs. I was secretly pining away for a different baby. I studied my hands in my lap. I was hiding my feelings about my daughter from the world. The old man in the doctor's office seemed to know better. Did Polly?

I read somewhere about how a girl with Down syndrome handled ridicule in elementary school. A boy was making fun of her at recess, "Hey Mongol. Mongol. Mongol." The girl, who was in fifth grade at the time, looked at him and said, "At least I'm not an asshole."

Sitting in the cold car, balling my eyes out, I had a moment of clarity. I was going to try very hard not to be an asshole.

"Mom? Mo-om. Mom!"

I heard a muffled voice behind me as I hurried through Wal-Mart. I had to get home for a therapy appointment soon, but I paid attention to the voice because I recognized it from long ago.

Jamie Hanson was in the middle of the aisle, turning around in a circle, searching for her mom. I hadn't seen Jamie for years, and I hadn't seen an adult with Down syndrome since Polly was born.

She was wearing tight denim jeans and a rock and roll t-shirt. Her short, boyish haircut framed thick glasses. Her jaw went slack when she wasn't calling for her mom.

I wasn't ready to talk to an adult with Down syndrome. I was just warming up to the idea that I had a *baby* with Down syndrome. But I knew this girl, and she was lost and frightened.

I went over. "Jamie?"

"Yeah?" Jamie turned towards me. She inspected me up and down.

"Jamie, it's Gillian. You know, from Napier youth group at church?"

She stared at me for a few moments longer and then her eyes lit up with recognition.

"Gillian! Oh my. Hi, Gillian!" Jamie pulled me into a hug. Her short, plump body was clammy. She had a wide smile when we broke apart.

"It's been a long time since I saw you last, Jamie. How are you? Are you lost?"

She looked around again. "Mo-om? Mom!"

"Jamie, we should wait here. I'm sure your mom will notice and come back to get you. Okay?"

"Okay, Gillian. I guess… I can wait here."

"Good. I'll wait with you."

I stood next to this woman with her rock music t-shirt and pixie cut and considered that she was my contemporary. She scanned the store for her mother while I tried not to stare at her.

"Jamie! There you are!" Jamie's mom, Marie, strode up to her daughter.

"I told you to keep up with me. We don't have much time. You may not stop to look at things without telling me, Young Lady."

"Sorry, Mom."

"I know you are sorry, but you had me worried."

"Mom, look. Gillian!" Jamie pointed.

Marie stopped scolding and glanced over at me.

"Gillian? Oh my goodness, Gillian!" She smiled as wide as Jamie had. "I have been praying for you. Julie called and told me about your baby." Marie took a step towards me and gave me a hug. She whispered in my ear, "I was thinking you needed to bring that baby back to the States." She stepped back but kept holding my arm.

"Jamie was frightened. She thought she lost you." I put on a big smile, hoping Marie wouldn't notice the fear in my eyes. I remembered feeling bad for Marie when I was in high school. It seemed like a lot of work to care for Jamie.

"And Jamie knows she needs to stay with Mom, right, Jamie?"

Jamie glanced at her feet, then sheepishly up. "Right, Mom."

"How are you guys? Is the baby here with you?" She peered behind me.

"No, she's at home. I'm just picking up a couple things. We're doing all right. We've started Polly in Early Intervention and are getting ready to tackle the list of specialty doctors she needs to visit."

"Oh, I remember the doctor appointments," Marie blew out her breath in a quiet whistle. "It's so involved at first, isn't it? You'll find that as Polly gets older, the visits will slow down. Of course, you'll have new challenges to deal with. Right Jamie, right?" Marie reached out and nudged Jamie on the shoulder. Jamie had been staring off but squealed with laughter at her mother's teasing.

"How's the baby's heart?" Marie asked.

"Okay. She doesn't have any issues. We're thankful for that."

"That's good. Real good. Now, listen, Gillian. I know this is hard for you. Having a baby with special needs is difficult. Believe me, I know. I did it in the 70s. Can you imagine? There wasn't Early Intervention or special schools or anything. I had to figure out how to help Jamie all by myself. I fought for her education."

I felt like I was staring my future in the face.

"I know it doesn't seem like it now, but with time, you'll see the blessing in your child."

You're right. It doesn't seem like it now.

"When I was younger I grieved the fact that we would never be empty nesters. Now, we make vacation plans and our first inclination is to include Jamie. We're the three amigos. Right, Jamie?"

"Right, Mom!" Jamie sang out. She turned and smiled at me. "Gillian, I'm so glad..." she stumbled over her words, "to see you again." Jamie reached out and gave me another hug. Her arms clung to me. Her embrace was tight. This time, my body relaxed against hers. *What is so scary about Jamie?* I hugged her back.

"We have to run now but please keep in touch. I'd love to help you in any way I can."

"You've already helped so much, Marie." I gazed at Jamie. "You have no idea."

19

"Are you going tonight?" Sergei asked.

My friend Megan had invited me to go to Pilates class with her in the basement of a neighboring church in town. Polly was now seven months old.

"You should go. It would be good for you to get some time away," Sergei urged.

I didn't want to go. Megan was in great shape, a beautiful mother of two. I had talked to her earlier in the day. "Oh, come on, Gillian. It's Pilates in a church basement. We'll be the youngest ones there!"

Megan loaned me a yoga mat and picked me up at 6:45 p.m. Pilates focuses on strengthening a person's core. You stretch and hold, lift and flex your way to a trim build. After my c-section with Polly, I would have to go searching for my core. My middle was like Silly Putty®. I needed the exercise and I needed to learn how to breathe again; to find ways to relax that didn't include bottles of wine and excessive sleeping.

At the class, I was put at ease after a few grandmotherly types squeaked and hissed from their backsides during the opening stretches. Once my giggles subsided, I lay on my stomach and peeled my head and shoulders off the mat.

I thought about Polly. Of all the therapies she started, physical therapy was her least favorite. We were supposed to put her on the floor for *tummy time* at various junctures throughout the day. "Her core is the most important thing right now," her physical therapist told us.

There I was, on my tummy, trying to strengthen my core and I felt close to my daughter. For the first time I was in tune with her, feeling what it would be like to reach the milestone of head control. At that moment, I willed her to have the strength to lift her head and look around. I willed myself to find strength as well.

One morning a few weeks later, I was playing with Polly during tummy time. She tracked toys from left to right and gazed at her black and white baby animal book. She still couldn't hold her head up for long, but seemed more interested in trying.

At first, she searched for me and when I wasn't in clear view she made do with glancing at the rattle and book near her face. When that got boring she started to cry. As she cried, she lifted her left arm up in the air. She waved it back and forth, like she was in a car and had stuck her hand out the window to hand surf. Only she was trying to get off her tummy.

I watched her struggle. On the one hand I wanted to be her savior. I wanted to swoop in and pick her up, cradle her in my arms and tell her everything was okay. But then I wondered what she would do stuck in that mess all by her little old self.

She fussed and fought for about ten minutes. Every few minutes her hand would go up high enough to tip her back. She looked like she was reaching up from the depths of despair. There was no more hand surfing; her little arms now punched into the air. "Curse you, woman!" I imagined her saying and I thought, *Go for it, Girl!* Then she would plop back to her tummy and return to fist pumping. Just when I couldn't stand it any longer, her hand and leg both shot upward, together. Her whole body sort of flopped over, and she ended up on her back. For a second she stopped crying as if to say, "What the heck?"

Then she screamed like she'd been poked with a needle. I cheered and clapped and cried happy tears. Polly had rolled over for the first time.

20

Our year in the loaner house was coming to a close. After going back and forth for months about it, Sergei and I decided not to return to Ukraine. We told the organization that sent us to Kiev that we wanted to stay in the States for three to five years because of Early Intervention therapy and medical care. Polly would need monitoring by an endocrinologist for her thyroid. The ophthalmologist said an eye patch might be in her future if her left eye did not strengthen with glasses.

But the real reason we were staying was because of me. I couldn't imagine moving back to Ukraine when having a child with special needs was still so painfully foreign.

So Sergei took a job as a Pastor at a small, struggling church on the North side of Chicago, and we moved from Michigan to Chicago in July of 2007. By then, Polly was sixteen months old.

If I were to show you a photo album of the next six months, you'd see pictures of Sergei standing in front of a church sanctuary, preaching to a handful of people. You'd see Elaina and Zoya posing all jazz hands in front of their new school, three blocks from our house. You'd see Polly sitting up in a Bumbo chair and reaching out to pat a monkey's soft ear in a board book. There'd be another picture of her with a cheeky smile that held her pink glasses up on her nose.

And you'd see several pictures of me. There would be one where I'm bringing my hands together with all my fingers curved into a C shape, signing "more" and trying to get Polly to mimic. You'd see me driving to and from baby therapy sessions and helping the girls with their homework. You'd see a picture of

Polly in my arms, eyes locked to mine. And you'd see me sitting alone in the living room, in my favorite brown arm chair passed down to me from my grandparents, praying to be a good mother to Elaina, Zoya and Polly.

Most days, fear still consumed me but it had changed. I was no longer scared of Polly, but I was scared *for* her, for both of us. I wrung my hands over the future. I walked around the house everyday waiting for something else to happen. When one in 691 live births result in Down syndrome, odds didn't seem much like odds anymore. I'd heard about other occurrences—say, one in 150 kids developing autism—and was convinced that would be us too.

I drove myself crazy worrying about Polly's health and future development. Would she graduate from high school? How much did she look like she had Down syndrome? What if she had medical complications? Kids with Down syndrome are more prone to Leukemia. Some kids with Down syndrome have infantile seizures. I watched Polly, judging her cognition and social skills, speech and muscle tone. Could she bring her hands together in mid-line? Did she make good eye contact? Was she babbling at all? No matter how much I processed, no matter how much I prayed, I still picked the worries right back up.

Sergei went to work and I settled the family into the house. The girls started school and Polly's in-home therapy schedule was set up in Chicago. We told Elaina and Zoya they could each pick one after school activity to go along with their first semester in their new school. Zoya chose ballet and Elaina chose gymnastics.

I went online and found classes that would fit into the family schedule and then dutifully sat at my computer the morning of registration, ready to hit the buy button at nine o'clock sharp in order to secure a spot for each girl in her chosen class.

The first day of gymnastics I waited outside Elaina's class thumbing through a book I wasn't interested in reading. The book wasn't that good. Another mom sat next to me with a book that appeared to be more interesting than mine. I asked her about it and we chatted for a few minutes. She chuckled at my dismay when I overheard someone mention that the gymnastics class was for experienced gymnasts; the look on my face gave away that Elaina was a beginner.

"Oh well, she's going to have to act like she knows what she's doing," I said under my breath. The mom next to me laughed again. I thought she was nice.

The next week, a rainy Tuesday, Sergei had a meeting so he wasn't able to watch the other girls while I took Elaina to class. Off we all went: Elaina, Zoya, Polly and me. I had a headache and Polly was fussy because she hadn't napped. Zoya decided spur of the moment she wanted to take gymnastics instead of ballet, so she was jealous. We shuffled up the cement stairs and into the building. Polly straddled my hip. Her coat was unzipped and falling off, and her hair was coming out of her ponytail.

The class was an hour long and I dreaded holding a squirming Polly on my lap for the duration. We couldn't play outside because of the rain, and the floor looked too dirty to let a baby roll around on it. Polly still wasn't walking.

The nice mom with the good book walked in a few minutes later. She noticed us.

"Hi, you're the minister's wife, right?"

I was surprised. Most people who know that Sergei is a pastor tend to avoid the topic.

"Yes, how did you know?"

"I'm Sarah, Charlie's mom."

My mind flashed back to a few months ago here in Chicago, right after we moved. Sergei had come home from the park with the girls and told me he'd met a lady who wanted to talk about Polly. She, too, had had a child with Down syndrome but her son had serious health issues and had passed away.

"She gave me her phone number and wants you to call her," Sergei said when he got home.

I was scared to call but I'd dialed anyway. Waiting while the phone rang, I looked out the living room window. The Japanese maple tree in the front yard was in full leaf.

No one answered and I left my name and number after the beep. But a few days later, Sarah called back. She and I talked about Polly for a while. I covered our history: lived in Ukraine, had Polly, spent three weeks in the NICU, sixth day a blood test confirmed Down syndrome, six weeks later we were on a plane headed back to the States. We talked about Early Intervention in the area and about a few therapists she recommended. I wrote down names and numbers on a piece of scratch paper.

Then I'd asked about her son and she began to cry.

"He had a lot of things going on. His little heart couldn't take it all. When we found out he had Down syndrome, I told my husband we could handle it. I knew we would have struggles, but I didn't consider Down syndrome a big deal. His health issues were something different entirely."

After Charlie died, Sarah started a preschool in his honor called Charlie's Place. The goal of the preschool was to provide a safe learning environment for all children. Sarah's dream was to see the preschool integrate typically-developing kids and kids with special needs, so they could learn from each other.

That evening, sitting in the dining room in the dark talking to a mother whose son had died, I said something I still regret, "It's taken me a while to grieve Polly's diagnosis." The air left my lungs once the words were out of my mouth. This woman was grieving her child's death. She couldn't hug him anymore, or kiss the insides of his elbows, or hear his laughter as he swung back and forth at the playground. I was ashamed. Sarah was living life despite her great loss, and I was walking around the neighborhood feeling sorry for myself, pushing Polly in a pink polka-dot stroller, while Elaina and Zoya led the way with the brightly-colored helmets, peddling their new bikes as fast as they could.

And now she stood in front of me while little girls hurried past us all a flutter of tights and slicked back hair buns. Her arms were empty, while I felt every ounce of my baby's weight in my grasp. Polly reached out to Sarah, who scooped her up without hesitation. I stood and watched as Polly nuzzled Sarah's neck. When their eyes met, I saw pain meet joy, thanks to my daughter's almond-shaped eyes.

In Chicago, we fell into our old family routines. Sergei was no longer home all day and I worked at bringing normalcy back into our lives. I wasn't hanging out in the basement getting drunk, or crying on the couch all day. The girls went to school and were allowed to watch one television show on PBS when they came home. They'd get a snack, and I'd help them with their home-work. When Sergei came home from work at about five o'clock, we'd eat dinner together. Afterward we would spend time together as a family and then get ready for bed.

Soon, we started a fun new tradition. On Friday nights, we'd pile pillows on the floor and get lost for a couple hours in movies like *Cheaper By The Dozen, Chitty Chitty Bang Bang,* or *Stuart Little*. Sergei would turn off his cell phone, and no one would talk about chores or homework assignments or bedtime.

My favorite part of movie night was the end of the movie. The credits would roll, jazzy music would start, and Elaina and Zoya would pop up and dance around with wild abandon. They were serious dancers. They'd peek out of the corner of their eyes to check if Sergei and I were paying attention. If we were, they'd laugh and shimmy more, maybe throw in a quick twist to wow us.

By now, Polly could sit up unassisted, and Elaina and Zoya lured her into the performances. She'd rock back and forth, back and forth, and laugh and smile, pleased with herself and her new motion. Elaina and Zoya keyed in on her, announcing that it was Polly's dance solo and we'd all watch as our baby girl would sway. After a few months of having family movie night, Polly—

close to a year and a half old—started to hold out her hand to stop her sisters in mid-motion. She'd then coax them to mimic her moves instead of imitating theirs. Pretty soon all three girls were doing the baby version of the electric slide. I would sit and watch in awe. Sisters. So much alike.

"I can't wait until I'm a grown up," Elaina said one day while we were out on a walk. "I want a cell phone. I want to eat as much dessert as I want." *You're right, you do get a cell phone when you grow up,* I thought. *You also get a job and bills and laundry. And often times you forget how to let loose and have fun for fun's sake. You forget how to jump up and dance at the end of family movie night without a care in the world.*

I've watched a lot of wonderful movies as an adult, the kind that make your heart stand up, jive and do the two-step while your bottom stays planted in the seat. For some reason, as an adult, I'd forgotten how to dance. My daughters were showing me how again.

Elaina and Zoya continued to teach me valuable lessons. I watched them and how they loved Polly. I tried to learn from them. I bought a book online called *We'll Paint the Octopus Red.* It's a story about a little girl whose brother is born with Down syndrome. With her dad, the girl makes a list of fun things to do with a sibling once the baby comes. Then, after they learn the baby has Down syndrome, she and her dad figure out that with help, the baby will do everything on the list. Elaina and Zoya were so young, five and six and a half, but they understood the message in the book.

"Down syndrome means Polly will need a little extra help, right mom?" Elaina stared at me as she talked.

"She can still do everything, right mom? And we love her, right mom? We'll help."

Polly was Polly to them, Down syndrome or not. They simply didn't care.

Time rolled on like a plastic ball lost in the street, and I was the kid standing on the sidewalk, wishing someone would come along and get it for me. The temperature dipped as we tumbled into fall. The leaves on the Japanese maple drifted down to the ground.

We went back to Michigan to celebrate Thanksgiving with my family, and then it seemed like I blinked and we were decorating for our first Christmas in Chicago. Our two-story house with slanted, old wooden floors and tall ceilings was ready for the holidays.

One day, a couple weeks before Christmas, Polly and I were spending a lazy morning at home while the girls were at school and Sergei was working next door in his office. There wasn't a therapy session scheduled. It was noteworthy—a day without the awkward existence of therapists in our home, singing out commands, and urging Polly to put multi-colored blocks in a bucket with the promise of bubbles. Polly still wasn't walking, but she was able to crawl around the house and pull herself up on the couch to cruise. She wasn't talking yet either, but she had a way of making her needs known through grunting, pointing and sign language.

The Christmas tree stood in the living room, in the middle of the large window. I love Christmas trees. As a little girl I'd lie under the tree for hours, staring at the inside sparkle of the lights—shiny, bright, blurred from my intense gaze.

I had turned on the white lights as soon as I'd woken up this particular morning. Our tree was like a patchwork quilt: a handful of wicker angels and reindeer; yellowed, unmatched ornaments purchased from thrift stores; trinkets the kids made at school; and cream and gold bulbs, all pulled together with a velvet red tree skirt that didn't quite lay flat. Christmas lights were strategically tacked around doorframes in our living room. A cheerful ceramic winter village was fashioned on the bookshelf. The twinkling living room lifted my spirits on that dark, winter morning.

Polly was happy. She had a full belly and a fresh diaper. Dressed in lavender pajamas, and wearing her tiny pink glasses, she crawled up on the couch and lured me into playing with her. I didn't feel like playing. There were many other things I should have been doing, like washing dishes and vacuuming. The beds upstairs weren't made and there was a load of laundry that needed switching in the basement. And deep down I was frustrated with myself for feeling sorry, once again, that Polly had Down syndrome.

But Polly kept putting herself right in front of me, smiling. I reached out and tickled her belly. Her little body erupted into a boisterous laugh. She sounded like a forty year old who had been told a dirty joke. This chuckle was new and made her entire body jiggle. In spite of myself, I started to laugh too, which made her laugh even harder.

Our laughter escalated into a mild hysteria.

My shoulders relaxed. I hadn't even been aware they were tense. The pressure I'd grown accustom to since Polly's birth, at times lessened by bits of joy and comfort, was gone. What was this new light?

Polly started to babble and I joined in. We formed a secret language on the couch near the Christmas tree. I was her sympathetic friend, listening to her unload her feelings. She'd coo, "Ah," like, "I'm feeling good today," and I would answer, "Ah?" Like, "I'm glad to hear that." Then she'd get honest. "Ah," which I know sounds similar to what she said before, but she was actually saying that her week wasn't going well, she hadn't been able to poop, and she was sick to death of tummy time. She didn't have the desire to work on her core strength. It was too much work. To that, my "Ah" affirmed that her life was difficult.

Not wanting the connection with my daughter to end, I flipped on some music and scooped Polly up. We swayed and watched the lights flicker. Our living room became an underwater universe and Polly was sharing her oxygen mask with me. I breathed her in for the first time, without feelings of fear or regret.

Sure, I already knew I loved her. Over the last twenty one months I had been poked and prodded along to love her by her sisters' immediate acceptance and love, by her deep sighs while she slept, and by the way Sergei protected her from the cold on a walk, bundling her up in the front pack with a blanket draped over her head. But this day was different.

On this morning, something deep inside me cracked open: unabashed love, thick like wet clay. I gathered it up for us and squished it around. Polly grabbed and flung it to me. I balled it up and sent it, once again, to her. It went back and forth between us all morning. Her smile, brighter than the Christmas tree, lit up her little face. We were lost in mutual adoration. This was what other parents to children with Down syndrome meant. "Let the baby change you." I'd gotten nowhere regarding Polly as a child with Down syndrome, but when I was able to see her as a baby, as my baby, a light switched on inside.

I thought about the words I had taped in my journal after we found out in Ukraine that Polly had Down syndrome. "The sun will shine again." I had wanted to believe them, but at the time it was impossible. How could my stunned, cold heart ever have felt the warmth of a love as bright as the sun? But now, sitting on the couch and playing with my sweet daughter on an ordinary morning two weeks before Christmas—the time of year when everything freezes—it was happening.

Polly giggled and flirted with me. I held her close without any barriers and closed my eyes. She forgave me with little chubby hand pats on my back, that told me she didn't love me any less for my tardiness. Her unconditional love warmed me deeply. Behind her sat our Christmas tree full of gleaming lights and trinkets and ornaments. At the tip of that tree was a golden star.

22

Winter thawed. I packed sweaters and long pants into gray plastic bins, careful to keep items Elaina and Zoya grew out of that still had wear in them—things like winter coats with matching fleece hat and glove sets. Then I put the labeled containers away for the future.

Polly turned two in April. I did her hair up in Princess Leia buns and my parents came from Michigan to celebrate with us. She was more interested in the wrapping paper than the presents. A therapist found us a toddler walker, which gave Polly freedom to walk up and down the street without help.

Polly handed out hugs and kisses to family and friends. Her dark blond hair grew down her back. She had physical, occupational, speech, and developmental therapy once a week in our home and started to tolerate hard work during sessions. She wanted to succeed at her goals. Her determined little mouth scrunched up close to her nose as she concentrated on pushing the walker forward with her forearms and coercing her legs to follow. Her muscles were still weak, and she was nowhere near walking independently, so we added another session of physical therapy at a center outside the city. Polly started to use more sign language to communicate. She picked up new signs every day.

My daughter was like small sips of hot cocoa, warming my limbs, bringing sweetness to my soul. I no longer thought about Down syndrome every day. Grief packed up his bags and told me he was going hitchhiking across the country, though he promised to send postcards. I morphed from a frightened new mother of a child with special needs into a knowledgeable mom, ready to fight for my child's rights, aware of the latest therapy and treatment options, and up on the newest medical check list pertaining to Down syndrome. I watched the therapists to ensure the best therapy for Polly.

In the fall, Zoya learned how to read; Elaina was known in her class as a good helper; and Polly started going to preschool two mornings a week at her therapy center. Sergei and I went away for five days to celebrate our ten-year wedding anniversary while all three girls stayed with my parents in Michigan.

Soon I was once again unpacking warm weather clothes: shorts and t-shirts and light cotton nightgowns. I washed things and folded them into dressers upstairs. The girls needed a few new items: bathing suits and bright white sandals. I watched them play in the parking lot between our house and the church during the long, summer days while I coaxed Polly to take steps up and down the sidewalk.

Things weren't perfect. I still had doubt and fear but the thoughts were fleeting. After Polly's birth, I used to wonder if I would always tell people right away that she had Down syndrome. A year into living in Chicago, it wasn't an issue. Sometimes I would tell a new acquaintance that I was the mother to a child with special needs, but most of the time I would say something like, "Hi, I'm Gillian. I have three girls: Elaina, Zoya, and Polly."

23

One rainy day, Elaina, Zoya and I visited the Museum of Science and Industry in Chicago. The exhibits were amazing: a man-made tornado, a coal mine that "transforms" you into a miner from the 1950s, and Christmas trees from almost every country in the world. But we found ourselves standing in front of a small warming space enclosed with plexiglass, watching baby chicks hatch from their eggs. We couldn't tear ourselves away. There were countless exhibits to experience at the museum, but we stayed there. We wanted to see a birth.

One egg was stirring like it would hatch soon. Every time it tipped and rolled, we would all *ooh* and *ah*, like we were watching fireworks on the Fourth of July. My heartbeat quickened. Elaina scooted herself up to the front of the little crowd that had gathered. Zoya grabbed my hand and squeezed it. After the first crack in the egg, we all went wild. We rooted for the chick. *Come on, baby! Come out and meet the world!* And when a hole was wide enough for the little scrawny, wet head and pointed beak to push through, we cheered.

What is more miraculous than birth? What a beautiful way to be born. In warmth and safety, with a crowd of people cheering for your life.

I wished I could have given Polly a birth like that. I wished she'd had some place warm to come into the world. I wished she'd been cheered for, smiled at, and loved from the moment of her first breath. I wished for a do-over. I wanted to do her birth again. I would wake up the morning after her birth in Ukraine, thankful for the gift of a child. I would be more present and open-minded. I wouldn't cringe when I heard about the possibility of Down syndrome. I wouldn't make snap judgments that imagined a little girl standing off to the side of life staring blankly with her tongue sticking out, as if that defined the quality and pleasure of her life. Instead, I would imagine my daughter: an adorable girl with sassy, hot pink glasses, who loves music and has a keen sense of humor and the desire to be a good friend. If I were allowed a do-over for Polly's birth, I wouldn't run to my bed and curl up into a ball upon hearing her diagnosis. Instead, I'd bend down and place my hand on her chest and vow to love and protect her. I would thank God for her. I would assert that even though difficulties would arise, I would be privileged to be Polly's mother.

Sometimes I deem the beginning of Polly's life as my saddest failure. I'm embarrassed by my lack of faith, my self-centeredness, and the direction I took to get away from the pain. I'm embarrassed that I didn't fall in love right away with my daughter. I know of other mothers who have children with disabilities, and right away they loved them and decided to fight for them. That isn't my story.

24

Polly is now five years old. She speaks in full sentences. She can run and jump. She is a great mimic. She loves to tell knock-knock jokes without punch lines and presumes she can do cartwheels, but, really, she just crumbles to the ground and pops back up. She laughs with anyone laughing and will give you a hug if she sees you cry. One night, not too long ago, I stretched out next to her for a moment at bedtime.

"Mom, sing…"

Polly likes it when I sing to her before she falls asleep. I lay my head against hers and stroke her thick hair with my fingers. I reflect about how I was afraid to lean close to her when she was born. I consider how she was formed inside me. She is who she was made to be.

I sing, "You are my sunshine, my only sunshine. You make me happy when skies are gray." I stop for a moment to clear my throat.

"Mom, more," Polly urges.

"You'll never know dear, how much I love you. Please don't take my sunshine away."

"More," she whispers again when the song finishes.

Her little hands that just recently lost their baby pudginess are cupped into the letter C and brought together. *More* is one of the few signs she kept once she learned to speak.

More, she signs, drifting off.

Will this little girl ever know she is my breathing sunshine? *Yes, my love. There will be more.*

Epilogue

The nose of the airplane pointed towards Kiev on June 8, 2009. We were returning to Ukraine, but not for boxes of keepsakes and clothes. We were going back to adopt a child named Veronika who had been abandoned at birth: a child with Down syndrome, who we would call Evangeline. A sister for Elaina, Zoya and Polly. It was no storybook adoption, if adoptions ever are. I did not feel love at first sight when we walked into Baby House Number 2 to visit the little girl we had chosen. I could not connect the love I had built up in my heart throughout the months of dreaming of her, to the child presented to us. I did not judge her mother for giving up her parenting rights, for in my own way I had once abandoned Polly. And upon meeting our new daughter-to-be, that revisited me. It was very hard. I faltered again and again before I could embrace this disheveled foreign child who seemed to hold no beauty. But that is another story.

*At the orphanage, a child cried in the hallway. A woman's voice demanded, coaxed, and reassured, "Toup, toup, toup, **step, step, step.** Come on. Let's go meet your Mama and Papa. **Veer-ron-eeeka. Gotova?** Veronika, are you ready?"*

Thanks

As a reader, the first thing I do with a new book is open up to the acknowledgements. I study names and close my eyes, imagining the author painstakingly attempting to recall every person who helped birth the book. I am shocked it is my turn to acknowledge all those who helped birth my own story into the world.

To Sandra Savage, thank you for finding my story, loving it, fighting for it, and making it immensely better. To L.L. Barkat and T. S. Poetry Press, for taking a chance on an unknown writer, and for turning my words into art. To my agent and friend, Sarah Joy Freese of the WordServe Literary Agency, I am indebted to your loyalty, hard work, and encouragement. Thank you for your voice of reason during my times of writerly despair. To Kate Hopper and Kelley Clink, who edited the first and second drafts of this manuscript. Kate, thank you for telling me this book had a place in the publishing world, and for pointing out the omission of one of my children in a key part of the narrative. Kelley, you are a writing warrior and a genuine friend. Thank you for being the phone number I dial with a writer S.O.S. To Annette Gendler, who let me into her advanced memoir workshop at Story Studio Chicago, when I really should have started in the beginner class. To my classmates in the workshop, thank you for critiquing my work. Without learning the art of critique and revision from you, I could still be sitting in front of a blank screen staring at a cursor. To my writing group: Barbara Coe, Sandy Suminski, Stephanie Springstein, and Kelley Clink, you are courageous, beautiful individuals and fantastic writers. Every time I'm with you I feel like I am sitting at the cool table at lunch. I'm fortunate to call you friends. To Bethany and Ben Fort, Amy and Wayne Giacalone, Jason and Kelly Gallagher, Jill Leblanc, and Rachel Osbourn, I count it a privilege to run in the same circles as you. Thank you for weighing in on my work, and for talking all things literary and artful with me at church. And a special shout out to Amy Giacalone, you are a cherished friend and a kick-ass writer. Thank you for driving me to that one publishing meeting and waiting for me in the car while I changed into a dress in the McDonald's bathroom. To my group of mom friends who pitched in and gave me a gift certificate to a writing class: look what you did! To my online communities: the Down syndrome forums, writing groups, my fellow pws, those who read and comment on my blog, and social media friends, thank you, thank you, thank you for your presence, however virtual, in my life. Thank you to Lisa Morguess and Lisa Peele for your reader feedback and the influence it had on the final version of the book. I would be remiss if I did not acknowledge our team in Ukraine who walked the real life story found on these pages with our family: Jim and Liz Baker, James and Julie Lauderdale, Lydia and Dennis Bowen, and Oksana and Dave Elsinger. Our three and a half years together in Ukraine are some of the best years of my life. To Christine Pinalto, you are good at making me look nice in photos. I owe you! Thanks for our budding friendship. To my bosom friends, Ginger Bowling and Andrea Bult, although it didn't make it in the book, you both found a way to call me in Ukraine in the hospital after Polly's birth. Thank you for loving me, making me laugh, and helping me grow for life. Special thanks to the congregations of Christian Fellowship Church in Chicago and The Chapel in St. Joseph, Michigan. I am happy to be a part of communities who strive to love God and people. Thank you for supporting our family through the years. Thank you to my family in Ukraine, Tatiana, Kolya, and Sasha, and to my dear friends who are close to my heart: Alyona and Raya. Special thanks to Lena, Elaina and Zoya's Ukrainian nanny who cared for the girls so well. To all the different people who showed up in this story, thank you for being such an important part of my life. To my sister Amy, thank you for being a true friend and a constant support. To my brother Justin, for making me laugh and being the first person to read this book in one sitting. And thanks to my brother-in-law Bill, and my sister-in-law Kris, and my nephews and nieces Will, Karli, Ben, Eli, and Kendall. To my parents, Karl and Anne Bayer. You are consistently in my corner even when I do crazy things like move to Ukraine. Much of the good in me comes from you. I love you. To my daughters Elaina, Zoya, Evangeline and Polly. The greatest privilege of my life is being your mom. Elaina, you are beautiful, compassionate, and smart. Zoya, you are funny, tender, and kind. Evangeline, you are a blessing from God. Polly, you are my sunshine. Thank you, girls, for changing my world every day for the better. To my husband Sergei, remember the other night when I told you a story in bed while we were falling asleep and we laughed so hard we woke up the kids? It's times like that, fifteen years into our marriage, that I realize just how fortunate I am to have you. Thank you for rearranging your work schedule so I could write, and for your continued encouragement and advice. To say that I love you doesn't quite seem like it is enough. I hope it is. And thanks be to God, for calling my name when I was fifteen years old.

End Notes

Chapter 4

Page 36.   "Myth: Down syndrome is a rare genetic disorder. Truth: Down syndrome is the most commonly occurring genetic": (Accessed online at the National Down Syndrome Society). <http://www.ndss.org/Down-Syndrome/Myths-Truths/>.

Chapter 5

Page 41.   "One book in the pile caught my eye. Jewel": Bret Lott, *Jewel* (New York: Washington Square Press, 1999).

Chapter 10

Page 61.   "Down syndrome: For New Parents, a site dedicated to helping new parents understand Down syndrome": (Accessed online at Down Syndrome for New Parents). <www.downsyn.com>.

Page 61.   "When you think you have learned what you need to know in life": ibid.

Page 62.   "The caption read: 'The chromosomes of a boy with Down syndrome. The arrow points to the extra chromosome 21.'": ibid.

Chapter 16

Page 87.   "I opened to Psalm 84, then underlined a portion: Even the sparrow finds a home there": *The ESV Bible: The Holy Bible, English Standard Version* (Wheaton, IL: Crossway, a publishing ministry of Good News Publishers, 2001), page 526.

Chapter 17

Page 92. "I had read about the growth chart and common medical issues in the book, *Babies with Down Syndrome: A New Parent's Guide*": Karen Stray-Gundersen, *Babies with Down Syndrome: A New Parent's Guide* (Bethesda, MD: Woodbine House, 1995), pages 63 and 105.

Page 93. "The best way to understand Down syndrome—what it means to your baby and what it means to you—is to get the facts...": ibid, page 1.

Page 93. "What is Down syndrome...": ibid, page 2.

Chapter 21

Page 116. "I bought a book online called *We'll Paint the Octopus Red*": Stephanie Stuve-Bodeen, *We'll Paint the Octopus Red* (Bethesda, MD: Woodbine House, 1998).

Also from T. S. Poetry Press

Rumors of Water: Thoughts on Creativity & Writing, by L.L. Barkat

A few brave writers pull back the curtain to show us their creative process. Annie Dillard did this. So did Hemingway. Now L.L. Barkat has given us a thoroughly modern analysis of writing. Practical, yes, but also a gentle uncovering of the art of being a writer.

— Gordon Atkinson, Editor at Laity Lodge

Booked: Literature in the Soul of Me, by Karen Swallow Prior

Prior movingly and honestly tells a compelling story of self-discovery through some of the greatest books ever written.

—Eric Metaxas, author of *The New York Times* Bestseller *Bonhoeffer: Pastor, Martyr, Prophet, Spy*

The Whipping Club, by Deborah Henry (an Oprah selection)

Multilayered themes of prejudice, corruption and redemption with an authentic voice and swift, seamless dialogue. A powerful saga of love and survival.

—*Kirkus Reviews* (starred review)

T. S. Poetry Press titles are available online in e-book and print editions. Print editions also available through Ingram.

tspoetry.com

CPSIA information can be obtained at www.ICGtesting.com
Printed in the USA
LVOW11s1511310716

498493LV00007B/662/P